Ernie

Hemingway's Sister "Sunny" Remembers

Madelaine Hemingway Miller

Foreword by Robert Traver

Printed in the United States of America

03 02 01 00 99   5 4 3 2 1

ISBN 1-882376-68-4

All photographs, except as indicated, are from the private collection of Ernest H. Mainland.

Cover illustration courtesy United States Postal Service. Used by permission.

Holt, Michigan

Contents

Contents (cont.)

Preface

I'm proud to re-release my mother's book about her brother. She resisted the urging of others to write this book for many years. She felt there was only one literary success in her family, and anybody else writing under the name of Hemingway was just trying to "cash in" on Ernie's talents. She held those same views for non-family members writing about her beloved brother.

This book was a labor of love for Mother. She toiled first in longhand, then started pounding on the old Underwood that was given to me when I went off to college. My four years at Central Michigan University did not wear out the typewriter; there was plenty left for her book.

I remember when she proudly sent off her manuscript to her editor, Nick Lyons. I also remember when it came back bearing the message that effectively said, "Nice outline, when are you going to do the book?" That was when she knew she was in for a piece of real effort and would find out just how hard it is to write.

In this reissue, I've added a few pictures that there was no room for the first time, along with a list of books in the libraries at Windemere and in Oak Park that might give clues to the early reading habits of Uncle Ernie.

This loving bio of Ernie by his sister Sunny, when taken with the other two "sibling biographies, presents, in my view, a candid look at the forces and family that shaped his life's work. I'm pleased to make Sunny's book available to a new generation of students and admirers of Ernest Hemingway.

—Ernest H. Mainland
April 1999

Acknowledgments

Of all the acknowledgments I have ever read, I have never seen mention of credit due an author's doctors and dentists, those who helped to mend and to preserve him. So I mention first, and with sincere gratitude, my favorite professional men who have helped me these many years in Illinois, Tennessee, Michigan, and Florida. I have outlived some of these men, all of whom tried their best to preserve me to this moment. Without mentioning their several specialized skills, they are: Dr. Cleveland J. White, Dr. Michael Holehan, Dr. A. H. Parmelee, Dr. Gerald Drake, Dr. J. E. Henri Simard, Dr. John R. Kelly, Dr. Ben Blum, Dr. E. Charles Price, Dr. Robert Dean, Dr. H. M. Matllers, Dr. Martin Roche, Dr. Charles Butts, and, more recently, Dr. E. K. Edwards and Dr. Tom O'Keefe.

To these, I add my unlimited thanks to many friends, relatives, and neighbors who not only encouraged but actually prodded me to complete this project. Among my friends, I give special mention of Professor Matthew Bruccoli, who first suggested I attempt this book of remembrances, and to C. E. Frazer Clark, Jr., who backed him up vociferously. I also thank my longtime friend Mrs. Charles R. Boynton, who read my first pages of notes and encouraged me to continue.

I wish especially to thank my friend John Voelker, better known as Robert Traver. It was he who convinced me that I should let these memories and pictures be published during my lifetime. I also appreciate his entrusting me to his present editor, Nick Lyons, whose skill and guidance brought forth this volume from my material. In short, I am grateful to every person whose life has touched mine.

—Madelaine Hemingway Miller
1975

Foreword

Though I lived for a spell in Oak Park, Illinois, during the early Depression years, and there began my own writing after marrying an Oak Park girl, Grace Taylor (who summered and still summers in northern Michigan "Hemingway" country), and through her got to meet Ernest Hemingway's mother and youngest sister (and still later, the author of this book and still another sister), and fished up in Michigan with Ernest's uncle, George Hemingway (and pumped him about his gifted nephew and my newest literary hero), I never did get to meet the man himself. For by that time Ernest Hemingway had long since deserted his native village and flown off to such exotic places as Paris and Africa and, still later, on to Spain and pre-Castro Cuba.

This failure of our paths to cross seems all the more a pity because the longer I know the author of this book, the more I wish I'd gotten to know her brother Ernest. I say this because old friends of the family have more than once told me that of all the Hemingway children, "Sunny" and her Ernie—as she still calls him—were the most alike in temperament, gusto, and charm. Still others add that Sunny more nearly reflects the sunny side of her complex brother. In any case I do know that my friend Sunny fairly crackles with all of these attributes and could, I swear, single-handedly charm a cuckoo out of an unwound clock—not to mention a preface out of an overwound fisherman during the height of trout season.

Literary critics disagree over many things, of course, one of their most rhetorically prolific areas of disagreement being over whether the early life and background of a writer is important or even relevant in any balanced appraisal of his work. Yet, curiously enough, many of these same "anti-laundry-list" critics are among the first to proclaim that a writer's most significant and lasting works are but the mature flowerings of those

Foreword (cont.)

impressionable dreams and memories gathered only during childhood and early youth. Since the subject scarcely lends itself to disposition in a preface, perhaps I'd better get back to that pleasant chore.

The book that follows covers many facets of the crowded lifetime of Ernest Hemingway. But mostly it is the story of Sunny Hemingway Miller's memories of growing up in Oak Park and northern Michigan with her older brother. Her story is enriched throughout by a wealth of old family photographs and snapshots, few of which have previously seen the public light of day.

To say that Sunny adored her brother Ernie and still adores his memory is not to suggest that a worshipful little sister has now lovingly contrived an illustrated literary valentine. Instead I think she has written an exciting and humorous and remarkably candid book about the importance of being Ernest.

—Robert Traver

*For My
Mother and Father*

1

To Ernie, with Love

All my life, Ernest Hemingway was not only my big brother but also my best friend. He steadied me in shaky times, encouraged me to be myself, and complimented me enough to give me self-esteem.

My adored brother has always been my hero. Long before his acceptance and fame as a writer, he contributed greatly to my growth and accomplishments. Being overpowered to a great extent by the scholastic achievements of the three oldest Hemingway children—Marcelline, Ernie, and Ursula—I was inclined to feel inferior and not care about trying to achieve. Ernie, more than anyone else, tried to keep me in line by complimenting my particular talents—my sense of humor, joy of living, dependability.

When Mother and Dad were more than disappointed at my grades and lectured me sternly, Ernie would put in such comments as: "Don't you know this kid has something grades will never show?"

You don't forget support like that.

And it continued throughout his life. His loving interest and encouragement, through letters and phone calls, long after he had become an internationally famous literary figure, meant much to me over the years. I saved many of his letters and only wish now I had saved them all.

Not that I ever intended to write about our family. My joke, when asked constantly when I was going to write some straight stuff about the Hemingways, was always: "Not me. I'm one of the few white people who *haven't* written about Ernest, and I intend to keep it that way."

Now I am persuaded that there are details I can add to the total story of my brother. I'm particularly glad I have so many fine photographs for this book.

Above left: Grace Hall Hemingway, Hemingway's mother.

Right: Grandfather Ernest Hall.

Dad always took pictures of anyone doing anything that seemed interesting; Mother faithfully preserved these. For each child she started a baby book, pasting in photographs and other items of interest—like birth and birthday announcements—and writing a detailed report of Hemingway happenings at the time. These multiplied to become many "memory books"—and they have served me well as just that. It is good to be able to share these intimate pictures and details of my famous brother's life—and to have been encouraged to "talk in print" about what a glorious privilege it was for me to be one of the six children who grew up in this family.

I'm always proud to say I am Ernie's kid sister Sunny—or "Nunbones," the nickname he always had for me. For me he could do no wrong. No matter how pressed he was, he always took time to keep in touch with his kid sister.

And I, in turn, always stuck up for him at home, where I became his

Record of
Madelaine Hemingway's
Baby Days

Four Years
From November 28th. 1904
To November 28th ———1908

MADELAINE HEMINGWAY,
BORN NOV. 28, 1904.
SISTER OF
MARCELLINE, ERNEST AND URSULA
439 OAK PARK AVE.   OAK PARK, ILL.

ambassador to the family court. When news came of his divorce from Hadley, and later of his divorce from Pauline, and Dad or Mother got so upset, I tried to tell them how adoring females of all types made Ernest's life abnormal. Divorce was unheard of in our family, and Mother felt Ernest's frequent divorcing was a family disgrace. Both parents were proud of his ability as a writer, though, and they boasted publicly of his success. Their quarrel here was with his subject matter. Mother, who had a unique way with words, emphatically stated that Ernest was "bastardizing a laudable art." Such strong words—so seldom used in our family—were powerful.

I defended him then and can now only write about him with love—and cherish each remembrance, happy and not so happy.

This book is for him.

I raise my glass: "To Ernie, with love!"

Above: a page from Mama's record of my "baby days" with the announcement of my birth.

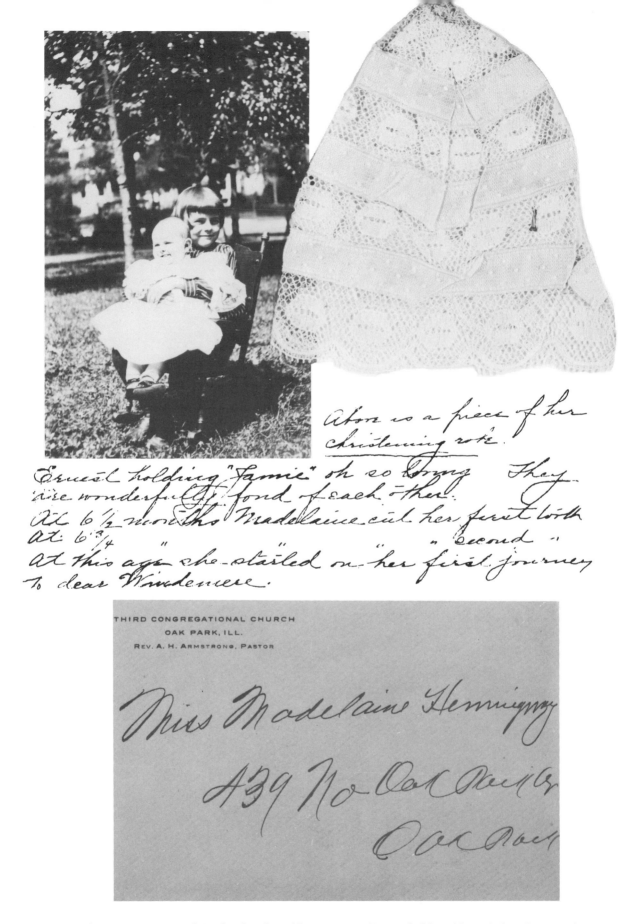

Above is a piece of her christening robe.

Ernest holding "Jamie" oh so loving   They are wonderfully fond of each other.

At 6½ months Madelaine cut her first tooth
At 6¾   "   "   "   " second "
At this age she started on her first journey to dear Windemere.

THIRD CONGREGATIONAL CHURCH
OAK PARK, ILL.
REV. A. H. ARMSTRONG, PASTOR

Miss Madelaine Hemingway
439 No Oak Park Ave
Oak Park

A page from Mama's record. Under the photo Mama wrote, "Ernest holding 'Jamie' oh so loving. They are wonderfully fond of each other." Attached to the page was a piece of my christening robe.

2

The House on Kenilworth Avenue

It is a lonely business searching my memories back through the many years since I was a child in Oak Park, Illinois, and, during the summer months, at Walloon Lake in northern Michigan. If only Ernie or Ura were alive to talk with—we three shared so many years of companionship—it would be easy to talk and remind each other of interesting incidents.

I remember our home in Oak Park vividly.

When my mother, Grace Hall Hemingway, drew up the plan and worked out the details of our Oak Park house, she and our father, Dr. Clarence Hemingway, planned on having six children. The location she picked was at the corner of Kenilworth Avenue and Iowa Street. At the time the cornerstone was laid on April 4, 1906, there were already four children. Marcelline had been born in 1898, Ernest on July 21, 1899, Ursula in 1901, and I, Madelaine, on November 28, 1904. We four had all been born in the house on Oak Park Avenue at the head of Superior Street. Carol was born at the Walloon Lake cottage in July 1911. Leicester, in 1915, became the only child born in the new home.

Our house on Kenilworth Avenue was unique in many ways. As an amateur architect, Mother was far ahead of her time, and the new house included many interesting innovations.

I remember the large, cement-lined fruit cellar, stacked with home-canned fruit and vegetables and barrels of apples and potatoes. Then there was a laundry room, with built-in tubs, and in it a gas hot plate where we sometimes saw wax heating before being set in molds and made into candles, or lead being melted to make bullets. When we children wanted to make some messy candy—

such as taffy—we were sent to the laundry stove where we wouldn't interfere with the routine upstairs. The workroom was a fascinating place, well equipped to build or fix all manner of things, and full of gadgets stored in boxes and trunks. There was a coal bin in the cellar, of course, often used by our pet cat for excrement; luckily, the coal—before it was shoveled into the furnace—turned out to be a deodorizer. There was also an area for the fireplace wood that was delivered outside and sent down a chute through a window.

The first floor had a large icebox and cupboard area in the hall adjacent to the large kitchen. Above the gas kitchen stove were skylights, and these opened up onto a small second-story porch.

The dining room had a large built-in buffet covering the south wall. Mother had saved many oil sketches painted by her mother, Caroline Hancock Hall, and she incorporated these twelve-by-eighteen-inch sketches into a frieze bordered with, and the pictures separated by, four-inch boards of walnut. The paintings were at about eye level and became immediate conversation pieces for anyone entering the dining room.

Below: Anson T. and Adelaide Edmonds Hemingway at the 439 North Oak Park Avenue House. Grandfather lived to eighty-seven and Grandmother to eighty-four.

I remember the big windows in the dining room, facing the back yard. We felt such joy when beautiful Jack Frost sketches surprised us there on a wintry morning. The dining room itself was large enough for an upright practice piano, along with the huge, round dining room table, with its many leaves stored away or extended for big family gatherings. The outside door in this room led to the back yard, porch, and another entrance to the music room. Beautifully designed leaded-glass doors, with a rose motif, led to the living room; these doors always had to be protected—and we children each learned early never to slam them.

And I remember the music room. The thirty-by-thirty-foot music room on the north side of the main house was two, then three, steps down from the living room. Mother had insisted that this room be engineered to have perfect acoustics, and it had; we always heard about her plan to add a big pipe organ, but that wish never materialized. The grand piano, numerous musical instruments, and later my full-size harp, together with oversized furniture, and a six-by-six-foot raised platform for singers or performers filled this room with elegance. It was especially beautiful at Christmastime, when Daddy would arrange to have a very tall tree from the Third Congregational Church festivities delivered to this room in time for us to trim.

The room was not without its hazards, though. After one buxom lady

Below: Grandfather and Grandmother Hemingway with five of their children–1917. From left, Nettie, Tyler, Clarence Edmonds, George R., and Grace. Will was in China.

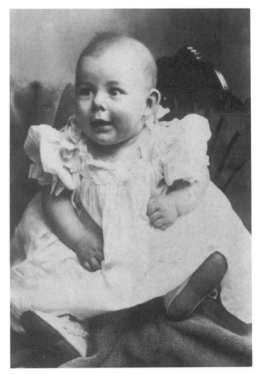

guest fell, not seeing the steps at the entrance, someone always had to be stationed there at large functions to warn the unknowing.

Above the steps was a balcony the length of the room, reached only from a landing near the second-floor level. The many folding chairs Mother needed for her recitals or musicals were stored on this balcony—which was also a lovely private place to hide or to be alone.

The living room was carpeted in a forest green that wore very well. It must have been able to take the abuse we all gave it, since this carpet was never changed in the twenty-some years I walked on it. The large red brick fireplace, with its crane and kettle, had an extra wide mantelpiece. Sometimes the big davenport was under the large front window that faced out onto Iowa Street, and sometimes seasonally in front of the fireplace.

The thick door leading to the vestibule was leaded glass. Two shields that Mother had designed were incorporated in it. They showed two clasped hands, a calla lily, and a shining sun—for friendship, peace, and happiness, Mother said. This door led to an outside door that was so thick and heavy that it once slammed during a windstorm and cut our poor pet cat's tail right off. There was the cat squealing under a chair on the porch and inside was most of his

Top: Our house at 439 North Oak Park Avenue, Oak Park, Illinois, in which Ernest Hemingway was born.

Bottom: 600 North Kenilworth Avenue, Oak Park.

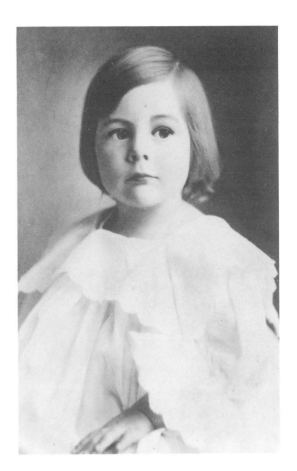

Right: Ernest Miller Hemingway as a young child.

tail. Thankfully he healed well after Daddy's expert emergency treatment. Whatever the cat had been christened escapes me, but from that time on he was known as Manx.

The adjoining library, filled with books and many stuffed birds and animals (Dad was an amateur taxidermist), served as a waiting room for Dad's patients. His office had a business desk, medical instruments in a cabinet, bookcases filled with medical books, and an operating table. The laboratory-lavatory closet harbored a full-size skeleton. Each of the children was allowed to take "Suzy Bone-aparte," as we called her, to school when we were in the right grade for such a study.

Since a great number of house calls were made in those days, Dad's office hours were very flexible. Often he'd see patients in the evening, and I can remember many times when he'd come out of the lavatory entrance and ask us patiently to quiet down: we never realized how noisy we were, either in play or argument.

The entire household was trained to answer the doctor's telephone intelligently and never to use the phone needlessly or for too long a time. We did

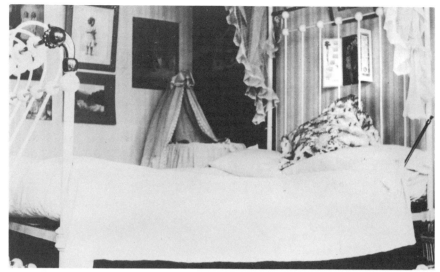

Left: Mama's bedroom and the bed in which we four older children, including Ernest, were born.

Below: Ursula (two and a half years), Marcelline (seven years), and Ernest (five and a half years) preparing to go sledding.

our best—but there were some hilarious mixups, like the time Louise Steffenhagen, our maid, took a message that Dad was to call the banker's wife when it should have been the Bankers Life Insurance Company.

On the first landing up the stairs from the living room was a huge mirror. I can remember how Ernie practiced his boxing on this landing. He would stand in front of the mirror and work very seriously, feinting and throwing punches—"shadowboxing" he called it. Sometimes he'd ask me to punch him in the stomach as hard as I could to prove how firm his muscles were. I'd do so, and he'd never flinch. The rest of the family, observing as we made funny faces at each other to extend the fun, were amused.

Mother and Dad's master bedroom held two three-quarter-size brass beds and bird's-eye maple dressers. There was also an outlet to a speaking tube that extended to the front porch. We'd whistle through it and then open a flap to speak.

Four other bedrooms were on this floor, and three more on the floor above. We each had a turn at each of them for our own.

Along with the maid's room on the third floor, there was a clothes chute that led to the laundry and a host of cupboards and storage drawers. After

Marcelline, Sunny on Dad's lap, Ursula on Mama's lap, and Ernest–January 1906.

World War I, we found one drawer filled with choice canned goods that Mother had stored away. We all had a good laugh when we noticed among her "survival" foods cans of lobster, crabmeat, and shrimp.

The house on Kenilworth Avenue was large and always full of activity. Each of us children was very individual in temperament and ability. Mother, who had studied to be an opera singer and later painted seriously, encouraged any artistic talents she spotted in us. Ernie always wanted to write. They soon

Below: Ernest, Ursula, and Marcelline holding Sunny, 1904.

Marcelline, Ursula, Mama holding Sunny, and Ernest, 1904.

Top: Ursula (three years old), Marcelline (seven), Sunny (six months), and Ernest (five).

Bottom: The music room at 600 North Kenilworth Avenue, including a copy of the Gainsborough painting of William Edward Miller.

learned that I had musical abilities. Mother, like Dad, expected great things from her children and always urged us to excel. According to our needs, we were given special instruction or necessary freedom. But Mother and Dad could also be sharply critical of our failures.

Though Mother loved all her children, she had very high standards of conduct and achievement that she wanted us to live up to. While we all did much that she wanted done, it sometimes seemed as if we could never really

satisfy her. Her criticisms and disappointment could show unexpectedly—and sometimes we thought unfairly.

Because we were all so different, arguments were common in our household, and we often took partisan sides. There were stormy times that took a good while to forget. We all thought, for instance, that Mother favored Marcelline, her firstborn, but none of us would use Marce's tactics of threatening to run away or kill herself if she didn't get what she wanted. Sometimes

Top: Ursula, Ernest, and Marcelline posing in a snowy yard–March 1, 1905.

Bottom: Dr. Clarence Edmonds Hemingway ready to go on calls in his "Tin Lizzie." It almost killed Daddy to give up the old pedal Ford. He so regretted the idea of the gearshift car.

Top: Ursula's fourth birthday–1906. (Left to right) Ernest, Elizabeth Hart, Marg Hall, Sunny (in front), Marce, Ursula, Edna Kuehl, Isabel Simmons, Howard Lyle Simmons.

Bottom left: "Precious Sunny" at two years and ten months old–September 1907.

Bottom right: Ernest Miller Hemingway at five years old.

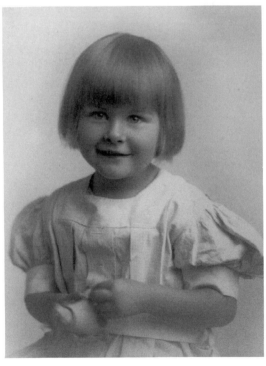

a rebellious child had to be disciplined, but love and respect for our parents prevailed during our early years, and their authority was rarely questioned.

Dad particularly enjoyed Ernie's companionship, especially teaching him much about folklore and the fine points of swimming, fishing, and hunting as well—which they did a lot of together up at Walloon Lake during the summers.

"We four"—Ernest, Ursula, Sunny, and Marce in grades six, three, one, and seven, respectively (March 1911).

Our happy family Thanksgiving dinner at Grandmother. A 29¾ lb turkey. We sang as usual at the table

My turkey 'tis of thee, Sweet bird of Cranberry Of thee I sing – I love thy breast and wings, back, legs, and other things – My mouth with water streams; Don't give me the neck. Tune My country 'tis

Sunny impersonated "Mistress Mary quite contrary" at a Mother Goose play. Nov. 27th. 1914

Ursula as "old Mother Hubbard at Mother Goose play

3
Up to Michigan

It took quite a bit of work and planning for our parents to get us up to Walloon Lake each summer. We packed big trunks with clothes and what seemed like necessities for a three-month stay at the cottage.

The stops the steamer made on Lake Michigan, at Ludington and Charlevoix, allowed us to greet old friends. Grace Taylor—now Mrs. John Voelker—and Elizabeth Harris—now Mrs. Alfred Aerne—used to be at the dock in Charlevoix while freight was being unloaded.

Before leaving Oak Park, we would each take on vacation some books from the Oak Park Library. And each of us who brought books was responsible for them and took that responsibility seriously. Ernie took the most books. I don't think he ever damaged one.

To this day when there is a thunderstorm or just a light shower of rain expected, my first impulse is to check outdoors. "Anything left outside?" rings in my ears from hearing it so often. But often there were slip-ups. I can remember finding a soaked book or pillow after a rain, and these books had to be accounted for, and paid for, which seemed fair to us all.

These vacation books became treasures, not only to us, but sometimes to a group of friends when we chose to have sessions of reading aloud. *Dracula* was a favorite one summer. Marvelously scary in parts, its horror was magnified when read, by kerosene lantern, to a group sitting around on the ground.

I was young to be included, but I remember one session. Ursula and I had planned to sleep out at the Point. But after the evening's reading, we both agreed, "Not tonight!"

If we came north by train, we usually brought some immediate provisions with us from the country stores at the foot of the lake. Crago's and Ransom's

Facing page, top: Mama wrote in her record, "Our happy family Thanksgiving dinner at Grandmother's."

Below: Sunny as "Mistress Mary quite contrary" and Ursula as "Old Mother Hubbard."

All Four Children on Ernest's Birthday July 21. 1905.

On Ernest's birthday with Mama & Uncle Lyley.

The end of July Madelaine took a very hoarse spell so she could scarce make a sound. We are having terrible trouble with her food. Mama can only nurse her 3 times in 24 hours, or once in 8 hours, and she refuses to take any artificial food — would rather starve. She is losing weight and running down — her flesh is all soft. August 2nd. Madelaine went to the farm with Mama, Papa and Sister Ursula for the first time. She went with us to a picnic on the farm August 5th. Emma worked an hour with her to force her to take 4 ounces of food. Sunday Aug. 6th She took 7½ oz of Mellin's in Walloon Village were well supplied to cover the basic needs. Then we'd go on up the lake to our cottage.

Later, when the boxes that arrived by freight on the Pere Marquette Railroad in Petoskey were delivered by horse-drawn dray, we praised the catalogue department of Montgomery Ward, which had a complete stock of produce in those days. Long before we left Oak Park, Dad had made out lists of what was needed; he always wanted to make life easier at our then-remote summer cottage. From Ward's we would get flour, sugar, ham, slabs of bacon, candy, cookies—gingersnaps were a favorite—cocoa and chocolate, and spices.

Many times we vied for the job of checking the bill of lading with Dad. That was the way to get the first look at the goodies that had arrived. But there was no fuss about who got what. Everything was everyone's, but was distributed only by the parents. With six eager children, careful distribution was necessary.

I still remember the joy of being allowed to pick from either peppermint candy or marshmallows. We were often rewarded with such treats for jobs well done.

Facing page: Mama's record of Ernest's sixth birthday, 1905. In the top photo Ernest (holding his "birthday gun") poses with Ursula, Sunny, and Marcelline. Bottom photo: We four children all pose with Mama and Uncle Tyley.

Below: Ursula, Marcelline, Ernest, and Sunny roasting marshmallows on our beach.

4
Settling In

The first chore upon arrival at the cottage was to take the shutters off the windows and pile them in the woodshed. Then Dad would climb the home-made ladder up to the roof to take off the chimney covers. These covers had big rocks on them to keep the wind, rain, snow, birds, insects, squirrels, and bats from coming down into the living room or the kitchen stove. Of course, the cover on the chimney for the wood stove in the kitchen had to be removed before a fire could be started for cooking. You only had to forget that one time. The lesson of the smoke and the grand cleanup stuck with you always.

After we had raked the yard and picked up the fallen branches, we were allowed to go barefoot. Then we could wander a little and savor the new clean smells of Walloon Lake. When you first arrived from the city, the lapping of the waves seemed so loud, but soon we got accustomed to it and listened to farther-away sounds and could see sights far off.

Shortly after we arrived, we were each assigned duties at the cottage. Ernie chopped most of the wood we needed and got very handy with the axe. But after a neighbor boy split his foot chopping barefoot, Dad made Ernie wear shoes whenever he went off to chop the chunk wood into stove-sized pieces.

Checking in at Bacon's farm nearby was an early joy. We made arrangements for morning and evening milk, and then we all took turns fetching it, along with fresh-churned butter and new-laid eggs, rain or shine.

Our icebox we kept filled from our own farm across the lake. Dad's joke answer when asked what he raised on the farm was "The best thing we raise is the flag." But we did manage to grow potatoes, vegetables, hay, and strawberries, and fruit was plentiful in the orchard. Ura and I were paid a small sum to pick potato bugs, which we dropped in kerosene-filled soup cans. We also pulled milkweed by the hundred.

Warren Sumner, for one, cut ice in the winter and packed it with sawdust in the icehouse there. We'd take ice tongs and a piece of oilcloth to carry it across the lake in our boat.

We always had either rowboats or launches to get about the lake. The launches we kept at Erni Culbertson's boathouse in the West Arm of the lake in the winter; the rowboats, and later our canoe, stayed in our boathouse. When the canoe was new, it rested all winter in the living room covered with a bed quilt.

The first few days at the lake we had to be on the lookout for deadheads, logs with one end waterlogged that often showed only a tip above the surface. These were very hazardous to boating of any sort.

Shore cottage owners were constantly on the lookout for good and not-so-good pieces of lumber or logs that washed up on the beach after an onshore wind. Many of the permanent docks from the West Arm down to the foot of the lake gradually came apart from ice pressures of the spring breakup. Their timbers were often good enough to build rafts and even diving platforms. "Finders keepers," we'd say when a good piece floated ashore.

Below: The original living room at Windemere. The window-seat boxes were also used for beds. Mother's hand-braided rug was made from old clothes.

The side yard and annex at Windemere the gate leads through a wood path to Bacon's. In fact Windemere is half way between Bacon + Murphy's.

Above: *The side yard and annex at Windemere, with Mama's description beneath the photo.*

Below: *Marcelline, Ernest, Harold Gore, Ursula, Jo Gore, and Sunny in the yard of Windemere Cottage.*

5
Getting a Canoe

The canoe was our treasure. Ursula and I had saved our own money to buy it, and in 1917 we ordered a green model from Old Town, Maine. We really wanted a red one, but thought it might be too conspicuous. The Old Town Company was out of the model we sent for but wrote that they had a red one ready to ship. Agreed!

When the notice that it had arrived by rail to the "foot" came, Ernie said, "Come on, Nunbones, let's get it."

We went down in the launch, named the *Carol,* but arrived just after five o'clock because the *Carol's* motor had rebelled. The station was closed, and there was a metal seal on the freight car.

The launch Carol *at Windemere dock.*

Ernie and I looked at each other, shrugged, and cussed a little. Then Ernie scribbled a note, broke the seal, left the note and our claim slip for the freight agent, and took the canoe. We carried it to the dock, tied a rope on it, and proceeded up the lake in a rough sea. It swamped a time or two, but we finally got the hang of how to tow it.

When we arrived at our shore, it was nearly dark. But the whole family welcomed us. We immediately tried the little treasure out— two by two, everyone taking a turn. Ura immediately named it *Bonita Pescada,* "Beautiful Fish," and we were satisfied that our challenge for that summer of 1917 would be to learn to paddle that canoe safely and swiftly.

Sunny and Ursula camping out at Murphy's Point– our favorite spot!

6
Indians

About one-half mile east of our cottage, there was an Indian camp, and since Dad, a doctor, had taken care of these lumber-camp Indians gratis each year, we knew a number of the Indians quite well—Nick Bolton, his son Richard (Ernie's and my friend), and Prudence Bolton, Rich's sister. Prudence was not good looking, but a good sport, and she tagged along with her brother sometimes, as I did with mine. Though some scholars hint there was something between them, I never saw any evidence of Ernie's liking her or even wanting her along on our exploring trips or squirrel-hunting jaunts. Stories! Stories! Then there was Billy Gilbert and his family, Billy Mitchell, and Billy Tabeshaw.

Ernie was always particularly interested in anything Indian. We loved to watch any of the lumbering projects that went on. Many times we were in the way, of course, when shouts of "timber" were heard, and the Indians pleaded with us to get on home, out of the way of danger.

It was also a fine thing to see the Indian women at work on their baskets and artifacts. They used sweet grass and porcupine quills very artistically. The women often came walking down to the cottages on a Sunday all dressed up, selling their baskets. The men of the camp had great regard for our father. He prescribed for them often, and they appreciated his many kindnesses and his ability, as did the people in the surrounding countryside and lake area.

We even loved the smell of the Indian camp. The odor of their camping grounds remained in the area for a few years after they had all pulled out.

One time Rich Bolton, Ernie, and I went exploring in the woods past the Indian camp. It was a long, hot walk, but I kept up with those two fellows so as to get in on their conversation. They talked about our nature findings along the way—fungi, tree moss on the south side of the trees, fishing, hunting, and stretching animal skins. Each shared his teachings from his father's knowledge.

When they started to talk about girls, Ernie told me to "lay back, we want to talk private." They didn't shut me out often, only once in a while, so I understood.

We came to a nice cold stream and, kneeling, I dipped my whole head in to cool off. I told Dad about that, and he said that was the worst thing I could have done. Just a little cold water on the forehead is safer when you are overheated.

Dad looked after us with every ailment, and his word was law.

He was very interested to learn what we had located of interest on our tramp through the woods and no doubt retraced our steps to check our findings later. His powers of observation were unique.

In the Petoskey area for many years a group of Indians came from Garden River, Canada, to portray Longfellow's *Hiawatha*. The pageant was held at Round Lake, north of the city, at a place we called Wa-ya-ga-mug. We sat on bleachers facing the small lake. Behind the bleachers the railroad tracks ran by on up to Mackinaw City. Coming into Petoskey on the "dummy" train from Walloon Village, after boating down to the village, was quite a trip in those days. And we were always impressed by the magical enactment of *Hiawatha*, especially when the young Indian dove from the high man-made cliff and later sailed off into the sunset.

Dad's visiting Indian, Albert Wabanosa from Canada, told us his grandfather had been Longfellow's guide when he gathered background for Hiawatha. He was an expert canoe maker and, of course, an expert paddler. He promptly showed Ursula and me the fine points of handling a canoe. We were taught the different strokes the stern paddler uses to steer the canoe and were shown how to paddle standing up and kneeling. Standing was often the way to reach shore when a quick squall came up and you were alone in the canoe.

Balance was essential, and he praised us both for our ability to adapt to it. We learned to "feather" our paddles expertly and could sneak up on picnic groups that took over the Point nearby and such favorite spots that we'd come to feel were our very own. "Squatters' rights," we called it.

We slept on the Point about a quarter of a mile from our home many nights, making beds in the open from cedar boughs. A fire to keep porcupines and skunks and other wildlife away cheered us on to storytelling and playing "truth."

7
A Game of Truth

"Truth" was a fine game Ernie introduced to bring out the good and bad points of one another's character and actions. Our guests for these sessions were carefully chosen. And before the session began, we all agreed to be sworn to secrecy. After we gathered over at the Point, a member of the group would be chosen to be "on the spot." This was always with his consent. The questions put to him or her were very personal. If the one being questioned refused to answer, there were penalties to pay—sometimes mighty harsh. One fellow I remember refused to answer questions about his girl. He was set afloat in a canoe without a paddle, at night, with an offshore wind. He managed to hand-paddle himself back to the group and got welcomed back and "off the spot."

This game was handed down to the group we had after Ernie left home— a younger crowd. Our penalties were more mild, such as gathering the firewood, or picking *five* gooseberries in the dark. The laughter got pretty boisterous at times, but there was no one near enough to be disturbed.

One summer Ursula and I got a little fancier by keeping an old bedspring at the favorite camping ground. After that, all we had needed to set up camp were the "eatments" and bedclothes. Everything was covered with dew during the night, but we expected that. Even so, every now and then it seemed we were compelled by the moon or stars to spend another cold, damp night out.

We used to sing songs, accompanied by my ukelele, making up songs and poetry. In those days we made our own fun. There were no radios, TVs, or cars to entertain us. It's hard to remember any of the words that came out, but I remember the shouts and laughter when Ernie contributed. When he joined the group, you could count on humor.

8

The Skunk Caper

One day when I was about ten years old, Ernie and I went across the lake to the farm. We were to bring back some ice, vegetables, and fruit. There was no hurry about getting back, so we explored the backwoods, which was virgin timber. Ernie carried his .22 as usual, and we climbed over fallen logs and branches and made our way pretty deep into the woods.

We came upon a clearing and then double-tracked back the way we had come. I was never afraid to go anywhere when I was with my big brother. His confidence became mine. Mother had said that when Ernie was a very young child, he would always say, " 'Fraid of nothin'." That attitude was his always— and it was contagious.

When we got back to the farm area, coming out of the woods, we saw a beautiful skunk near the old barn. Ernie shot it without hesitation. We talked over the matter of what to do with it. It smelled some, but not too terribly.

"Nunbones," Ernie said, "this skunk is too good to waste. What say we take it across the lake and plant it near the visiting campers at the Point?"

We felt they had stayed long enough.

"I'm game," I said, "but won't it smell up all our stuff on the way there?"

"Trust me, kid. We use this old pail and cover him with dirt and later sink the pail."

Facing page: A page from Mama's record with a photo of Daddy and Uncle Tyley and their catch of fish.

We stopped at the Point on our way to Windemere. It looked deserted. The campers were evidently off on some trip for the day. Ernie borrowed their shovel and buried the skunk behind their tent. I waited in the boat as lookout. When he came back to the boat, we had a good laugh and agreed never to tell anyone of the episode.

The campers left the next day. Ernie and I didn't wonder why.

She sits on the floor and amuses herself alone for quite a time, - can climb out of the baby carriage

Here are fish from Brevoirt Lake caught by her Daddy and

Uncle Tyley. She ate some - the very first solid food in her life

At 7 months she had her picture taken in over-hauls with the fish - also with her brother + sisters and the Gore children. - All in overhauls

She eats a little fish and bread but does not like it. She still fights against all artificial food and her poor Mother has scarcely anything left to nurse her with.

At 7½ months, makes a sniffy face and then laughs when ever we say "Sunny, can you make a sniffy face.

9
Ernie and Me

One day Ernie took me fishing for bass out in the bay. He had instructed me carefully in the art of casting, but our equipment was mighty primitive compared to what we have these days.

We took turns casting out as far as possible, letting the weighted spoon—with its red-and-white feathers and very sharp barbs—drag slowly through the water toward us. We did this over and over. Nothing!

"A bad day! The wind isn't right. The moon is wrong." Any of these comments seemed to fit.

Then, rearing back, I made a powerful cast that somehow hooked Ernie in his bare back, between his shoulders.

I was shocked and grieved.

"Don't be upset, Nunbones," Ernie said. "Take it out."

I couldn't. I knew I just couldn't do it—and there the hook was, deeply imbedded in his flesh.

"Cut it out," he ordered, his voice growing firm. Then he leaned over and handed me the old blade we sometimes used to cut bait.

"I can't, Ern, I can't!" I pleaded. "Please let's go to shore and have Dad get it out. Please!"

He grumbled to me that he could stand it, but finally agreed to row in.

When we reached shore, Dad sized up the situation, located his clippers, clipped off the now-protruding barb, and backed the rest of the hook out. "Now a drop or two of iodine will finish the job," Dad said.

When he'd finished, we cheerfully went back out on the lake. The next time I cast, Ernie did not say, "Don't hook me again." I appreciated that.

Another time we were exploring around an old building up the lake when

Ernie stepped on a rusty nail. We had all been taught that a rusty nail wound brought lockjaw. People could die of lockjaw. The thing to do first was to make the wound bleed, then suck the "dirty" out.

No question what to do here! Ernie couldn't reach the bottom of his foot to suck it out, so after trying, he called to me.

"Nunbones, how are you?"

"Fine over here," I said, "no excitement."

"Then come over here and help me. I can't reach my foot and I've stepped on a lousy rusty nail. There, see?" I looked. It was a nasty puncture. "You've got to get down and suck the bad stuff out. Don't swallow, just suck hard on the wound and spit out promptly. Can you do it?"

I told him of course I could.

We went through the process several times, and finally he said, "That's good enough, I think, just one more time for good luck."

Good luck we had. No infection set in.

Nowadays people are against such procedures, I understand. I guess our mouths had less germs in those days.

On an outing with Ernie to explore the shoreline up in the North Arm of Walloon Lake, we went ashore near Indian Garden to investigate. We were about to sit down when we noticed poison ivy all around. I had a great regard for the power of the trileafed ground cover; I'd once had an itchy rash from it. But Ernie laughed at me and said, "It's silly to let it have power over you." He often said things like that. He offered to eat a leaf of the stuff to show me he lead the power of resisting the poison.

I was horrified to see him swallow it.

I watched him carefully the next few days but he suffered no ill effects from the poison ivy. I broke out the next day on my feet.

Our nursemaid, Ruth Arnold, with us in our homemade bathing suits– 1912.

When I told my friend Hinie Grunde down at the boat livery at Walloon Village the next time down, he gave me the sure cure he used. It was one to three parts of sugar of lead and witch hazel. It's a fine cure. Hinie's beloved dog Rags used to bring poison ivy home regularly to Hinie after running free. Just a few welcome-home love pats brought the rash out for his master.

Though Ernie was always busy, he often had time for me. And our times together were always special, in one way or another. One time I remember we were playing catch in the yard at Windemere with a new hard indoor baseball. Not that I couldn't usually catch his throws—or he wouldn't have played with me—but this one time a hard-thrown ball hit me on the nose. This Hemingway nose, which I always say is just for smelling, was bent off side, and I had a bad nosebleed. Ernie was so solicitous and upset at hitting me that I couldn't let on how much it hurt. Daddy appeared and pulled my nose back straight and we all quieted down with assurances and comfort from Daddy that I was really okay. Ernie let me play catch again as soon as the bleeding stopped so I wouldn't feel too badly. He didn't blame me for not catching the ball. He blamed himself for not throwing it correctly.

What a guy!

Top: Ernie and a large trout–at seventeen.

Bottom: Ernest at seventeen with his catch at Windemere–on the shore is the new canoe.

10
A Weekend at Horton's Bay

One time—for a special treat—Mother let me go with Ernie to Horton's Bay for the weekend. I stayed at the Dilworths' and Ernie stayed with friends. To get there, we rowed across Walloon from our cottage to our farm area. Then, tying the boat securely to a tree and hiding the oars down the beach, we picked up our small extra clothing sacks and tramped on foot over the rutted, sandy road.

We had to hike about three miles, but, talking and joking all the way, it didn't seem far.

The Dilworths welcomed me and showed me the room I was to have.

Mother and Mrs. Dilworth both painted landscapes, sometimes together, sometimes apart. We younger children were always welcomed at the Dilworths' and at the blacksmith shop owned by "Uncle Jim" Dilworth. Uncle Jim would let us watch him shoe horses, and when he wasn't busy at the forge would let Ursula and me use the big bellows to make horseshoe nail rings and such treasures. And the Dilworths had a big rope swing to enjoy, and there were often kittens to play with in the barn.

Mother painted a scene of the roadway looking toward Uncle Jim's blacksmith shop. This landmark is now long gone. And later she painted a lovely picture of the church in Horton's Bay where Ernest and Hadley were married. The church, too, has since been torn down. But the old country store is still standing and many of the residences of old Horton's Bay are well kept up.

I remember one beautiful shoreline marine picture Mother painted of Pine Lake—since renamed Lake Charlevoix—looking toward the area where Ernest and his friends often camped out and fished; after Mother died I gave that picture to Ernie's good friend Bill Home. The road down to the shore is about

Mother's painting of the blacksmith shop at Horton's Bay.

the same, though we used to see many lady-slippers and more wild flowers than are there now. The old, enormous dock at the foot of the road and the big warehouse we called the beanery, where Wesley Dilworth had storage, are also long gone. The big boats from Lake Michigan, such as the *Missouri,* used to land at that dock to pick up produce.

The shoreline looks different to me now, and the old, natural Horton's Creek that Ernie so often took me fishing on is unrecognizable. Word was that the property was bought up and "beautified." It was so wild and beautiful before, with the old dam and wildlife, that it seemed sacrilegious to change it.

Anyway, I settled in at the Dilworths' that weekend, and soon Ernie came back with his friends and asked me if I'd like to play baseball with them.

I was always honored to be allowed to join in his activities. Being the only girl with the four fellows didn't bother me a bit.

Ernie said he had boasted to his friends about my batting and pitching ability and that now was my chance to make him proud of me.

We had a happy time playing for a couple of hours in the open field, and Ernie told me I'd done fine. He was usually the only one of our family who ever showed he was proud of me for anything.

Ernie heard there was to be a big barn dance that night not too far away. He told me that he'd take me if I'd promise not to give him any trouble. So I promised.

After supper, I put on my Sunday dress I had brought for church. I tried to make myself look as good as possible, but I'm sure what was possible fell far short of good. Anyway, I was ready when Ernie and his friends called for me.

Aunty Beth Dilworth said she thought it was all right for me to go, but not to stay too late as she would be waiting up for me.

When we arrived, the music was playing loud and strong. There was a distinctive barn odor of dust and hay. I danced a bit with some of the younger boys, and soon I was a tired kid. It had been a big day. Across the floor, I could see and hear my brother and his group having some very noisy fun.

The next fellow that asked me to dance got a refusal. Maybe he thought I wanted to go out and sit in one of the cars, as so many had left the floor to do, so he invited me to rest this one out and get a little fresh air.

This sounded fine to me so, without telling Ernie, I disappeared from the barn and the crowd.

We hadn't got seated in the back seat of a car before Ernie came running out, hollering for me. When he found us, he grabbed the boy and began shouting loudly and wildly about my being just a kid and that he was my brother and responsible for me. He was furious.

The boy got the message and left the yard rather than go inside the barn and again perhaps enrage my brother. Already there had been a couple of fights in there, provoked by almost anything. The crowd was wild enough to enjoy watching any fight.

On the way back to the barn, Ernie gave me a lecture and sat me down near the fiddler; he told me firmly not to get off that chair until he came for me.

Horton's Creek, Horton's Bay, Michigan.

I could see I had given him trouble and guessed I had spoiled his evening. It wasn't long before he came to me and said, "Let's go, kid."

I told him I was sorry, and I meant it.

On the ride back to the Dilworths', Ernie lectured me very forcefully in front of his friends.

"Never," he said, "go out to sit in a car with a fellow unless you want to be necked. Never let a man press you against a wall, and never lie down on the grass."

His friends were quiet and seemed to agree with him on all counts, so I took the sermon very seriously.

Ernie told me not to tell anyone about the evening's excitement, especially the family. It was more than likely that he and his friends returned to the barn dance after they deposited me at the Dilworth home. I never heard about that. Before they left, though, Ernie made a date for us to go fishing in the morning down at Horton's Creek.

When I was trying to go to sleep, I realized how shaken up Ernie had been and how deeply he felt his responsibility as my protector. I didn't have sense enough to appreciate his concern; it seemed to me he'd made a big scene over very little.

After an early breakfast, we walked together down the narrow road to the dock area of Pine Lake. Then we went off to the right to locate the choice spots on the stream. All the way over, Ernie instructed me regarding being noisy or conspicuous when fishing for trout. He thought it best to wear dark clothes and make no unnecessary movements. Since he usually brought back a lot of fish, I trusted his advice and was sure he'd lived up to his own rules.

He placed me at a spot where I could cast my fly out a ways and let it drift down with the current past one of his favorite holes. I was told not to shout when I caught one, but to unhook it calmly and place it in my creel. Later, he said, we would compare our catches and see who'd gotten the most.

He left me and crossed over at the dam and without a wave of his hand, but still in sight, he started to fish.

A beautiful, quiet peace surrounded the area. I concentrated hard at casting the fly and watching it come down the current. Suddenly I saw a fish boil. I struck hard, lifted the struggling fish up onto the bank, and was just removing the hook from its lip when I saw out of the right corner of my eye an enormous snake come swimming downstream. It was all I could do to keep my mouth shut, but I did. That was the biggest snake I had ever seen. The hairs on my arms stood up and I tingled all over.

I said nothing, though, and continued to fish.

Later when we got together to compare our catches, I asked Ernie if he'd seen the big snake.

"Sure," he said, "he was nothing. Lucky he didn't grab your fly."

I told him, "You bet it was lucky! I sure would have had to holler for help. Would you have understood that, Ernie?"

He looked at me, smiled, and said, "Maybe."

We gathered up our gear and walked back up the road to clean and give the trout to Aunty Beth to cook for lunch. After lunch, we went over to the general store to see friends and buy some sweet goodies to take home to Windemere. That store was loaded with beautiful things. What variety! There was fishing stuff, wearing apparel, corncob pipes, bakery goods, and all flavors of pop. It seemed to me that they had some of everything there. The only problem was to find it.

Hiking back to Walloon, we stopped at the Sumners' to share our candy with the children. They gave us some fine fresh vegetables to take home.

While walking, we talked of many things, but neither of us brought up the subject of the barn dance. I kept expecting another lecture, but Ernie evidently had decided to let the matter drop and enjoy the last of our weekend together.

11
Life at Walloon Lake

We obtained transportation at Walloon Lake to go to "the foot" for provisions, or perhaps Eagle Island to dine at Mrs. Davis's wonderful eating place, or other stops through the years, by flagging down such boats as the *Tourist*, *Wenonah*, *Outing*, *Rapid Transit*, and others. I remember big docks built on rock piles at Lake Grove and Eagle Island in the West Arm area, Murphy's Point and Bacon's Landing in our area, and Wildwood Harbor diagonally south from our shore.

Then there was Echo Beach Inn (Johnny McConnel's) and Melrose (John's brother Henry's), now the Thomas Bakers' property. Farther down the lake was Indian Garden, the Pines, the Thomas House, and Walloon Village. You can still see some of the old foundations for these public docks if you know where to look. These spots make good fishing for bass and perch, but are hazards for boaters.

I was five years younger than Ernie and a tomboy in those young days, so I tagged along on his exploits and duties. He wanted me along.

I can remember going squirrel hunting with him, and how, after he shot a squirrel, he carefully skinned it and stretched and nailed the skin to a plank. He treated and cured the skins with salt and arsenic, as I recall, but I have no remembrance of what was done with them after all that. Once Ernie and I came home with a few frogs we had speared in the cove creek. I held the feet while Ernie skinned the legs—and when they were fried they nearly jumped out of the pan.

Together, we really made what we thought was a "fist full of money" peddling the extra fresh vegetables that grew on our farm across the lake from the cottage. We used our launch, the *Carol*, to take the vegetables around and had regular customers that had good enough docks for landing our launch. People looked forward to our now-and-then trips.

We sold beets, carrots, lettuce, and even ice to very special people. Being the younger, I did the footwork, running up to the house to see who wanted what when we landed. Then the people would come down to our boat and pick out what they liked. We let them set the price.

When Ernest became famous, some people boasted that he had been their "iceman."

Our family life was very close for a number of years. We shared constantly. Dad "palled" with any of his six children who loved the outdoors. He taught us to shoot, see the beauty of nature, share our joys with our friends, help those in need, and much more. We were taught to watch for chances to help anyone in distress on the lake—and towed many a boat to our dock!

We used the grassy hill next to us for clay-pigeon shooting. The small children graduated from pulling the trap to being allowed to shoot if they wished. These "pigeons," claylike round discs, came by the barrel from Chicago, and it was great sport for Dad and Ernie to show off their ability at hitting the sailing discs high in the air. Dad, using his favorite 12-gauge named "Old Ed," often got two shots at one disc before the pieces fell to the ground. This was his "show stunt." Dad taught Ernie to be an excellent shot and was

Ernie got this woodchuck at Walloon Lake.

proud of him. Each of his children was taught to handle guns. I preferred the 20-gauge to the 12.

Our mother made each of us conscious of the beauty of sunsets, waving wheat fields, and music; any artistic efforts we put forth she praised and encouraged.

And we always had pets of one sort or another. We used to get kittens from the farmers at the beginning of the summer. When one of these was sometimes loved to death, or accidentally killed by a pest trap set by Dad, we gave it a beautiful burial. A shoebox coffin held the remains, and the burial, complete with handmade headstone, took place in what we called "The Grave-yard" in our yard. We children marched around the gravesite with dignity, and the music of tinkling tunes, furnished by a hand-wound music box, didn't detract from the solemnity of the occasion. Dead birds got the full treatment, too, if they were songbirds. Crows that Dad and Ernie shot to cut down the early-morning noise we disposed of without ceremony.

When Ernie joined in these burial ceremonies, he did so with little enthusiasm. He just went along with Ura and me. Marce felt too superior to pretend.

◆ ◆ ◆

One day Ernie and Alfred Couch, a local friend, let me go along to the old

Left: Dad at the clay-pigeon range in the field next to us—a crack shot!

Right: Dad in fishing outfit in front of the Ursula of Windemere, *which had been towed to the head of the lake on the Crane trip.*

Our agreement concerning a "certain porcupine."

schoolhouse to look around. I spotted a big porcupine in the woodshed. Ernie and Alfred shot it, and we brought it home. Soon I realized I had no claim to the prize, for I was made to sign a statement to that effect. Why I had no claim escapes me now, but maybe it was a trade of some sort. We often made "deals" of various kinds, and "legalized" them with such formal documents.

Up in Michigan, Ernie, because he liked his privacy, slept in a tent beside the little cottage we called the Annex. He often read late at night—and wrote— and his light in the tent was on later than anyone's. I think, too, he fancied himself the "lookout" for all of us.

One night, when I was about ten years of age, after I had undressed and was ready to go to bed, my curtain somehow blew into the flame of my candle in the end room of the Annex. The flames drove me down to the main cottage—stark naked—shouting for help. Ernie grabbed his bedclothes and rushed from his tent to snuff out the fire in record time. It was very exciting for a few minutes, but after that I was not trusted with a candle for a long time. Our kerosene lamps and lanterns were safer and gave better light.

Fire was always a possibility, and help from elsewhere most improbable. A fire usually meant you were "burnt out," a total loss. Many of the hotels on the lake eventually burned to the ground.

In our early days at Walloon Lake, a brush or forest fire was a very serious and dangerous thing. There were no adequate roads to bring firefighting equipment from any town, so all able-bodied men, even guests at the resort hotels, helped fight fire. A house, cottage, or hotel that had a fire was usually destroyed. One time, I remember there was a bad forest fire. A signal was planned that the Siddens's test boat, the *Onward*, would come down the lake from the West Arm to warn us to leave our shore for the opposite side of the lake. We packed supplies and supposed valuables in the two rowboats and launches. The air was smoky enough for us to be forced to breathe through wet handkerchiefs for a while, but before we had to leave the shore, the fire was brought under control. Ernie and Dad returned, tired and dirty, after what seemed to us a very long time. We were grateful and relieved.

12
Windemere

Our cottage, called Windemere, was originally a twenty-by-forty foot building. Later the large screened porch and kitchen were added, and the former kitchen became a bedroom. As more children arrived, a three-bedroom building, called the Annex, was added onto the property.

During my dating years, a favorite beau spent quite a bit of the summer with us and was paid to reroof the Annex. He built a porch on it as well. A letter from Dad to Mother praised him for his good work. Dad said this was the first "star boarder" we'd had that had ever contributed anything.

The window seats on either side of the main-house fireplace were mattressed to serve as extra beds. The fireplace had a crane from which hung an iron kettle. Below was an Arkansas bakepan that cooked many a fine cornbread. The amount of wood that was cut to size and also chopped by hand axe for both the wood stove in the kitchen and the fireplace was enormous. The reservoir on the back of the wood stove was a fine source of hot water. But we did very little hot-water bathing during the summer; the lake usually served the purpose.

Ed Morford and Jake Rehkopf built the original cottage.

Whoever drilled the well did a fine job. The original well is still our source of clean, pure, cold water, as of 1974. One of the summers of "improving the cottage," we moved the hand pitcher pump from the side front yard into the kitchen and had a sink with a drainboard put in.

Each June the leathers of the pump had to be renewed and the pump primed at great length to get the well water started. But when it was past the new leather taste, this water was served to guests with all the ceremony of fine wine.

Top: "We six" and Daddy at Walloon Lake.

Bottom: The front porch at Windemere. Ernie is top right.

Sometimes, by seasoning our water with ginger, sugar, and a little vinegar, we made what was called "strong farmer's drink" or haymakers' switchel. This—Dad's concoction—seemed very special to us. I've tried making it as an adult, but it just doesn't seem to have the class it had as a childhood drink.

Iced tea and cocoa were also favorites of ours. No one fussed about the frequent lack of lemons for lemonade. We just couldn't expect it, and we accepted that.

Our marshmallow roasts and duck dinners—along with a barbecued young porker or two—were occasions to invite local friends to share. The Nickeys, who had a cottage on Eagle Island at the Narrows toward the West Arm of the lake, were frequent guests. We children were encouraged to call older folks who were friends of our parents "Aunt" or "Uncle" and "Grandma" or "Grandpa." We called our farmer neighbor Grandpa Bacon from the beginning.

Until he died in 1972, at the age of 102, I still saw one of Grandpa Bacon's sons, "Uncle Joe."

◆ ◆ ◆

The buildings on our property in the early days consisted of a boathouse at the shore, the woodshed, and later a chicken house of most original design—

Top: Sunny, Les, and Carol–the old boathouse and shoreline at Windemere.

Bottom: Some Hemingway cousins at Walloon Lake: (back row) Ernest and Marcelline; (front row) Franklin, Sunny, Virginia, Adelaide, Ursula, Jane, Isabel, and Margaret.

made from the big wooden crate in which the little piano that was an octave short had come.

When our parents had both died, Mother left Ernest the Windemere property; he, in turn, gave it to me with the understanding that it should never be sold, "except for dire need," and that it should go to my son, his godchild, Ernest Hemingway Mainland. So I had the woodshed, which had been a spot to put all unneeded but possibly useful articles for years, torn down. We found many choice things in the woodshed that the winter marauders had missed. We had to choose what things, such as ice tongs and fence stretchers, should be saved, and what must be discarded.

The woodshed had many memories for me. We were sent there for discipline when our table manners weren't what they should be. Ernie named his sitting place in the woodshed "The Throne," and hid some old magazines to entertain him while he put in his time there. He shared this secret with me. I was sent to the woodshed nearly as often as he.

The chicken house was gone by this time to make small hutches near the five-board fence that surrounded the property where Ernie, for a short time, kept small animals.

"Hemlock Park" outhouse, with sign printed by Larry Thomas (shown), 1971.

The door casings in our main house at Windemere still hold the measurements of our family and some friends. Some house guests were measured and their marks were signed and dated also. Each year we were instructed to stand

straight, barefoot, with a book placed on our heads, as a mark was made on the wood frame. How much we grew each year became a matter of great pride. The marks that were on the framework of the big front door were saved to frame the large picture window that was installed when the rotted front porch had to be eliminated in 1952.

"Hemlock Park" still remains. This, our outhouse, had great distinction. It was decorated with deer antlers and had a fine assortment of magazines and catalogues. "Hemlock Park" was a fine retreat when indispensable jobs were to be done. Recently, for a joke, my friend Larry Thomas made a sign stating, "Ernest Hemingway Sat Here."

"Our group"– with Mama–in the front yard at Windemere.

13
Neighbors

The Bacon family was always good to all of us. No doubt we were in the way a great deal, but they let us share in the fun of picking fruits, gathering eggs, milking cows, and riding on the hay wagon to bring in the hay. Sometimes when I hung around Carl Bacon while he was milking, he'd squirt me in the face while I held my mouth open to catch a little warm milk from the source.

But there seemed to be an understanding between the adults that we should never be allowed in the slaughterhouse. Of course, that made it intriguing, and we'd scheme to get a good look at what went on in there. But we never got in on anything gory. Maybe Ernie did, but he never told me.

Before the Bacons had a cream separator, the milk was wonderfully rich. You wouldn't believe the cream that rose to the top! Later, when market prices became known, the cream was sold separately, and we sadly noticed the change.

The excitement of being chased by a bull or a turkey gobbler, and the enjoyment of seeing the fluffy baby chicks keeping warm in the farmhouse kitchen were a big part of our summer's amusement and excitement.

Sometimes Carl and Earl Bacon—Joe Bacon's sons—together with Ernest, Marcelline, Ura, and me took any house guests we had to Sunday night service at the church in the valley on Resort Pike. We went more for social than religious reasons, I'm afraid. The building was torn down a while back, but the old schoolhouse that was adjacent is still there, housing hay; recently I noticed it has been made into a home and painted a cheery yellow. A huge lilac bush blossoms there every year. None of the one-room schoolhouses that I know of in this area have classes anymore, but some have been turned into very livable homes.

A page from Mama's record: (top) some of us with Mama posing with the Ursula of Windemere on Dad's forty-third birthday; (center) Mama with some of her children (Ernest and Marcelline had gone home to Oak Park to enter high school); (bottom) Dad and Mother with Sunny, Carol, and Ursula on Bacon's Pier going home to Oak Park, Sunny to enter fourth grade, Ursula to enter sixth.

Top: Ernest and Warren Sumner haying at Longfield Farm.

Bottom: July 13, 1915–the day after Wesley Dilworth's wedding at Windemere.

One night at evening prayer meeting, the preacher could not rest until everyone had come to the rail up front to confess Christ. The minister preached on and on, and all of us except Ernie and Hawsey, a friend visiting from Oak Park, went up front. The minister kept ranting about the wicked "resorters" who were fast going to hell, and we kept looking back at Ernie and his friend, who still showed no signs of rising to the occasion. Finally we motioned to him from the rail to please come forward. Ernie and Hawsey finally came down the aisle. They later said they were just testing the preacher's stamina—which was fine with us, except that we'd gotten awfully tired of kneeling at the rail. It was a few Sundays before we dared go back to that church.

14
The Blue Heron Matter

One day Ernie asked me if I'd like to pack a lunch and go with him to the head of the lake and explore. As always I was eager, and we were on our way in a few minutes in the launch *Carol,* towing our rowboat with *Ursula of Windemere* printed on her side. We went up into the head of the lake—the wild part—as far as possible, and then anchored the *Carol* and went ashore in the rowboat. Ernie had his gun, so we felt safe to explore.

Soon after we landed, Ernie spotted a blue heron and shot it. He said it would make a fine addition to Dad's collection of stuffed birds and animals.

"What say, Nunbones?"

"Darn tootin'," I answered.

Rather than carry it with us, he rowed out to the launch and wrapped it in papers, putting it under the seat for safekeeping.

When Ernie returned to me on shore, satisfied the hot sun would not spoil the bird, we tramped around to find a choice spot to have our lunch. Though Ernie didn't admire my aversion to snakes, he understood my nervousness when one came near our picnic spot—so we decided we'd had enough exploring and beat it back to the launch.

We got a mean surprise when we arrived: the bird was no longer under the seat.

We figured the game warden or someone had heard the shot and followed up to see what was going on. We had no love for game wardens; there seemed to be so many new restrictions pointed out to us lately as to what we could and couldn't shoot, and when, that we disliked everything and everyone connected with them. Before, a bird had always seemed logically ours if we could bag it.

Ernie and I decided not to tell anyone about the heron. Dad was down in

Oak Park on some special "baby case" at the time, so why should we tell anyone else? I don't recall that we thought we had done any wicked thing. We didn't even expect to get caught. But we were mad at whoever had stolen our prize.

The next day Ernie went over to the farm across the lake to help Warren Sumner with the haying. I forgot about the bird—until a man showed up at the cottage on foot inquiring if this was the home of a young man with a black and white launch and a rowboat named *"The Yurshula of Waldemire."* Mother said yes, but the rowboat's name was *Ursula of Windemere,* correcting him in her grand manner. The man identified himself as a game warden and said he had come to arrest the young man for shooting a blue heron at the head of the lake, the area known then as "Cracken."

Mother bristled with disgust and ordered him off our property.

He refused to go.

So Mother said, "Sunny, go get the shotgun!"

I brought it out promptly, and with this the game warden left promptly, forgetting to shut the gate behind him but saying he would be back.

After a quick consultation with Ursula and Marcelline, who now got into the action, Mother decided to have one of them row across the lake to the farm where they should give Ernest the news and fresh clothes for him to go to Horton's Bay and consult Wesley Dilworth about what to do. Wesley advised him to go to our Uncle George's near the Ironton Ferry, or else he'd take him to Boyne City to see the judge and to confess.

They went to Boyne City. After Ernie told his story to the judge, he was fined some small sum and let off. This news a day or two later relieved us all, but the incident put a scare into Ernie and me we never forgot. He used the incident as the basis for one of his Nick Adams stories.

Our parents made little of the episode—no big "bawling out" that I remember. We had learned our lesson.

15
Another Sister

Our sister Carol was born at Windemere. Because her birthday was July 19 and Ernest's was July 21, we had a joint celebration. A pine tree was brought from the woods for a birthday tree. We all helped decorate the tree and made a gay, festive occasion of it.

In our family, we had not only a "tooth fairy," but a "birthday fairy." This meant that another child nearest the age of the real birthday child also got a present.

Thirty-six guests at Windemere for a barbecue on Ernest's eleventh birthday.

It's been said that Ernie was very disappointed at the arrival of still another sister, instead of a brother. If that was true, he never let any of us know his feelings. So far as I could see, he adored Carol as a baby and was very tender and sweet with her.

In adult life, he—like me—very much wanted a daughter. Instead, he had three fine sons, and I had one. It could be that his endearing name of "Daughter" to female friends he was especially fond of was a small satisfaction to him.

Ernest's eleventh birthday–Daddy, Mother, and four children "all dressed up."

Sister Carol was born at the cottage. Above: All of us bringing home her first birthday tree—1912.

Below: Ernest carrying his and Carol's birthday tree, with "Mother Gracie" seated, 1913.

*A page from Mama's record: Right,
Ernest on his fourteenth birthday,
displaying his catch. Below, "our group"
after a duck dinner. Mama's comment is,
"Oh so happy."*

*After the Duck Dinner
Oh So Happy*

16
Teenage Fun-and Nicknames

Besides our usual activities of swimming, hunting, boating, exploring, and the small duties we were assigned, we often had dress-up parties. Prizes were given for the most outlandish outfits for encouragement to, our friends. In teen-age summers, we had a group of friends from the Lake Grove area who entered into the spirit of this nonsense wholeheartedly. Katty Nulson, now Mrs. Richard Williams, and her sister Mary Orr McCarthy, Hazel Peaslee, and many others comprised the group of false-padded, jewelry-bedecked, lovely folk with enormous funny bones.

Our other nonsense included nicknaming. Our family gave Ernest and me the credit for designating nicknames for each of us. Marce was called Masween or Mash, and later Ernie called her Ivory. I called Ernie Oinbones. He called me Nunbones, but Sunny was like a real name to me then, and still is. Ursula we called Ura and sometimes Uralegs. Carol called herself Dee, then it got to be Deefish, then Beefish, until finally Beefy seemed like her real name.

Leicester, the youngest, was called Dessy at first, then Gaspipe and Currence. Ernie named him The Baron later—a name that stuck. Privately, Ernie and I spoke of him sometimes as the Monkey Buppus or Dregs, when we were using our secret language or lingo.

Nicknaming people became a habit. Sometimes the names were descriptive, but always they were humorous—and rather senseless. I loved to vie with Ernie as to what was the best nickname.

Ernie used the whole business of making up nicknames in his early stories— and used imaginative nicknames all his life.

In our teens we spent many hours wandering over the hills and through the woods. We'd find choice sticks that we would whittle to make fancy walking canes. The path from Bacon's Farm through the woods and over a few streams to Indian Garden was a good long walk. Sometimes we'd cut a basswood or willow stick and make a whistle of sorts. Of course, no whistle could take the place of our family whistle, quite like the call of the bobwhite.

We also had a unique call, the sound of which could be heard a very long distance over the hills or on the water. It was: "Hip ta milika, honigazock, to boom ta la, to you whoo!"

If you heard that, you answered: "Chip ta wasta, king da basta, hibble de hibble de, you whoo-oo-oo!!"

I have no idea of the origin of this call, but I have hollered that sometimes in the wide open spaces to see what might happen.

Ernie and I found, in the woods on the way to Echo Beach, a tree that as a sapling had bent down; somehow the top had grown into the ground. We suspected the Indians had made it as a trail marker. It made a beautiful natural arch, and we always made a wish as we walked under this growing freak of nature. We guarded it and showed it with pride to visiting friends on our walks. It was a sad time when we came north one summer and found it had been broken down by another fallen tree.

Because there was so much untouched timber and ground cover, the wild flowers were more profuse and seemed to last longer. When Dad walked with

Sunny, Carl Edgar, Bill Smith, Charles Hopkins, Mother, Ernie, Ursula, and Marce.

us, he'd teach us to recognize the gems of the woods and fields. There was a patch of spearmint between the Melrose Hotel and the Indian Garden Hotel.

Indian Garden Hotel, at the beginning of the North Arm of Walloon Lake, sported fancily dressed ladies all glittering with jewels, who came from many

Left: Ursula, Ernest, Sunny, Carol, and Marce on a raft that Ernie and I made– 1912.

Below: The Indian Garden Hotel at Walloon Lake, from a postcard.

states. That was the exclusive card playing group, or porch-rockers. The Ellis family owned that beautiful spot for many years. It was quite an occasion when we went there by boat for a meal.

Often we went berrying for blackberries, raspberries, and wild strawberries, wearing rough clothes, such as overalls, that were semi-briarproof. Before the present tree farm was planted behind our cottage, the best patch of strawberries was there. Mother enjoyed our jaunts and took part happily until some bees or other insects would send her home. We each carried our own berry pails and constantly vied with each other not only to pick the most but save the most to bring home. The rewarding taste of homemade jams and jellies made the hot job of picking worthwhile.

I remember vividly how much fun we had playing Indian tag in the fields by the light of the moon at haying time. Our neighbors and friends joined in playing the game of hiding behind haycocks and trying to reach "home" before whoever was "it" could catch you. A quick kiss now and then, while hiding waiting for a chance to reach "home," added to the merriment.

The full, or harvest, moon in August was the most brilliant, either in the fields or on the water. Many times when we were out on canoeing dates, we saw brilliant displays of the northern lights or shooting stars—"star brilliance" could entertain us for hours.

Ernie and Louie Clarahan crossing Lake Michigan on the steamer.

Sometimes we got so entranced with the peace of canoeing that before we knew it, a mist would rise on the water, obscuring the shoreline completely. If we didn't know the tree silhouettes, it was easy to get lost—even though not very far from home.

If the wind came up and we wanted to stay still and stop paddling, we'd tie

Louie Clarahan and Ernest (right), preparing for a trip to the Upper Peninsula.

the thwart of the canoe to the rushes that grew on the sandy drop-off point near shore. When the dating-canoe traffic was heavy, the broken-off bulrushes made the favorite parking spots obvious.

The Point was a favorite spot. That was first known as "Murphy's Point," then "Illinois Point," and now "Willard's Point" (because John Willard's home is there), which isn't quite accurate as the Worcesters and Marian Davis share part of the area on either side at present.

Top: Sunny and Cecil Dunn canoeing near our homemade diving raft.

Bottom: Ernest, Sunny (rowing), Paul Haase, and Ursula at Windemere–1915.

Across from our cottage and a little to the west was a flourishing sawmill in the early 1900s. Great booms of logs were towed up the lake by tugs to the mill. Later, when the mill shut down, the old pilings left near the shore made very fine bluegill fishing; casting there for bass is difficult because so many hooks get snagged.

There was also a good patch of watercress nearby that was worth getting your feet wet for. Ernie and I transplanted some of it on the Windemere side in the cove next to us. It flourishes today. In fact, it almost chokes the little stream that flows into the lake!

When cucumber time came, we all looked forward to Dad's making pickles. His cooking has been written about—unfairly—as though it were a pain to him. He adored it. He prided himself on his secret recipes that had been handed down from his mother. He soaked the pickles in brine in big crocks. I remember getting caught a time or two licking pickles and returning them to the crocks unwashed.

Dad also made the best fried cakes and pancakes ever. Our summer and winter cooks had to step aside when he got in the mood to cook. He would announce his intentions and follow through.

At cherry time, we kids took turns running the metal cherry pitter that was clamped at the edge of the oilcloth-covered table. These canned pickles, cherries, jellies and jams were shipped down to Oak Park in the fall, in barrels, well packed against breakage. We consumed them all winter and enjoyed the feeling of having helped make what we ate. Our fruit cellar at 600 North Kenilworth Avenue was a treasure chest, not only for our family but for gifts to friends and some of Dad's favorite patients.

17
On (and in) the Water

It was many years before any cottages or hotels on Walloon Lake had Delco-motor light plants. They were very noisy, but many liked the power that made electricity more than they liked the natural stillness of the area. We luckily didn't have any droning motors too near us for a long time. We preferred kerosene lamps, lanterns, candlelight, and later lamps with mantles that used gasoline of some fine nature. These lamps, when pumped up, made very bright light.

Our boat docks were very crude and slivery, made of cedar posts and scrap lumber. When too many pounds of people stood on the dock to greet or say goodbye to visitors, a board would often break and a skinned shin would result.

To be pushed off the dock was usual for almost any reason, especially if the time designated to wait before swimming after a meal seemed too long. The clotheslines were always full of wet bathing suits and clothes, and our early homemade bathing suits of flannel dried slowly. The later knitted suits were a slight improvement.

We all learned to swim at an early age. We made rafts for poling and also a diving raft, and our parents bought a good diving board plank at Zipps Lumber Company. But safety measures were drummed into us constantly. We were taught the power of the water, particularly when the wind was up, and we never swam alone. "Watch the sky," Dad told us. "You'll always have plenty of warning from even quick squalls."

The only close call I remember was when Leicester was very young. He and I were swimming when suddenly he went under. One, two, and by the time he would have gone under the third time, I was hauling him ashore. I held him by the ankles and shook the water out of him; fortunately, he was soon all right.

We older children and our friends were interested in long-distance swimming. One person always had to row beside the swimmer, and the time and distance were recorded. It was about one and a half miles across from our cottage to our farm. Ursula was the best long-distance swimmer in our family. Ernie, who swam for our high school, and Marce were next. I only made it to the Point one time.

Naturally any evening swimming was done "neenigh"—as we called naked. The air was cold, but the water warm, and it seemed as though without a bathing suit, you could swim much more easily and swiftly. There was no embarrassment and that way we could avoid putting on a wet suit. Towels and soap were available on the dock for anyone who wanted to bathe seriously.

This we called our secret society. All of us took part, though perhaps not all at the same time. And if any of us had guests, we respected each other's privacy.

Ernie out on Pine Lake. He wrote on the back of the photo, "Me trusty Birch Bark viacle. Length 9 feet wt. 20 lbs. Just as sturdy as a church, like hell. You have to part your hair in the middle to balance it."

The early days of the Yacht Club of Walloon were great fun, especially on racing days. Such motorboats as the Siddens's *Onward* and *Sneak*, Randall's *Mary Belle*, and Frenzel's *Muncie Meteor* were the classy boats. But the Johnsons' *Dad*, Mort Port's tub, Willard's boat, and Bruggeman's *Sandy*—and even our dory, the *Sunny*—were great drawing cards in the special handicap races.

The commodore I remember the best was Fred Adams. His cottage was where the Sayers and Henikas are now in the West Arm. He was the one who first took it upon himself to stake a marker and light a kerosene lantern on the end of the sandbar at the Narrows every night. This service guided boats through the Narrows and was greatly appreciated.

The Lake Grove Hotel was a flourishing, beautiful resort. No one who ever ate anything there, especially Mother Rehkopf's lemon pie, ever forgot it. The Lake Grove dock was spacious enough to be a social gathering place, as well as a good fishing spot. Everybody seemed to know each other, and hunting and fishing stories, as well as stories of boat mishaps, were exchanged. Ursula and I enjoyed telling anyone who would listen about the time the *Wenonah* got grounded in our bay while trying to land at one of our rustic docks. She and I made a big thing of diving down to retrieve the propeller while applause came from the passengers and captain.

My launch, on the day we christened her–1910.

18
Porkers

One year my father decided to have the experience of raising two little pigs. He built a small pen back of the boathouse and a shelter for our two squealing friends, named "Gar" and "Bage." Dad nourished therm all summer with the prescribed swill, in addition to our fresh garbage from the kitchen, with a planned outdoor barbecue in mind.

When they were big enough, the Bacons—appropriately named—butchered them. Dad dug a trench near the beach and fashioned fork-shaped sticks at each end to hold the porkers. I do not remember whether the spit was a metal pole or a green limb. Each of us took turns watching that the meat was turned and basted and the fire kept up for hours.

The finished roasts had an apple placed in their mouths. To the horror of Mother and some of the guests, they looked too natural.

Afterward, as on many such occasions, Mother played the piano and we joined in singing favorite songs. I remember singing such favorites as "Swanee River" and "Old Black Joe," and many hymn tunes.

19
A Midnight Party

Once Ursula and I carefully planned with our dates to have a midnight party. Because we had bought enough food for eight instead of four, we invited two other girls staying in the same cottage as our dates and then induced Ernie and his house guest to be their dates.

We had the food hidden in the cove next to our cottage, the pop in the cool stream, and the foodstuffs in a tin container. We all planned to go to bed as usual and around midnight, when everyone was asleep, sneak out and take the canoe and rowboat to call for our friends around the Point. Ernie went along with all these plans just to please Ura and me.

Everything went according to schedule: we picked up our friends, added their boats to the flotilla, and headed up the lake to our agreed spot on the sandy point of the Narrows entering the West Arm of the lake. The secrecy was the most fun, but it was a beautifully calm night and that made it delightful. That area was unoccupied at the time so we sang and carried on hilariously.

It was definitely a group party. We only paired off to return home. Arriving at Windemere's shore at about four A.M. we saw two ladies coming down the hill carrying a lighted lantern. Had we been found out? We learned the next day that they rowed over, woke Mother, and asked if their teenagers were with us. Mother told them she hadn't seen them and that her children were asleep.

But when they investigated, they found Ernest's tent unoccupied and our rooms empty. Their worries and aggravations grew to a fine state! At that point, Ruth, our housekeeper, whom we had taken into our confidence, had to speak up and explain where we were. The ladies left in their rowboat to return to the one young boy we hadn't invited. He had called in the night for attention and so revealed the absence of the other young people.

Nothing was said to us as we sneaked by the main house to go to bed, but in the morning the air was *blue* with condemnations and criticisms. Our innocent picnic was judged to have been a disgraceful orgy. Ernie and his guest were blamed unmercifully because they were older and should have had more sense. Ernie, Ursula, and I went promptly to the Loomis cottage to try to explain and apologize. Mrs. Loomis and the visiting aunt refused to see him. When Ernie reported that, Mother told him and his friend to pick up their belongings and go over to Horton's Bay, where they would work for their board and room until this matter blew over.

Quite naturally Ernie felt that he was being kicked out over nothing, but he left immediately. In time Ura's explanation of the event was accepted. Our punishment was the same as that of our friends who were involved: be in every night before ten o'clock for the rest of the summer. Sometimes we took an alarm clock with us to make sure the hour would not be set earlier, for in those days an ultimatum was respected.

The next summer I was sent to a girls' camp in Minnesota.

20
The Lake Changes

Walloon Lake changed very little until 1926, when Dad finally gave the county permission to come through our property to build a road from Resort Pike near the shore and through the woods on up to Lake Grove Hotel. The dynamiting of stumps and the noise of the road builders practically ruined that summer. When Ben Thompson's team of horses needed refreshing from pulling out stumps, he drove them down to the lake. He reminded me lately that one time part of his horses' harness dropped off in the lake and I went out to retrieve it for him. That makes us friends to this day.

Later the Bacon farm was sold to an out-of-towner named Roy Brown, and the designated roadway was changed slightly. Some land owners were deeded the extra piece of land that now lay between their original markers and some were not. As always, there were a few hard feelings that soon disappeared.

Our usual paths to walk through to the Bacons' were not as virginal now. The denseness of the woods and the special lights and shadows we used to see were changed. Before, Ernie and I hadn't felt conspicuous while spearing frogs in the cove creek. Now everything seemed out in the open. But Ernie was off on his own by this time—he'd been to the war and had already written his first book—so there was no one to spear frogs with anyway.

21
Home to Oak Park

By September we would have to pack up and leave Windemere and close the cottage for another year. Sometimes we were a day or two late for the opening of school, but generally we got back to Oak Park in time to start the school year.

Holmes School, our local grammar school, was just a block from 600 North Kenilworth Avenue. The high school was a good long walk from home. Often in stormy weather, Dad would plan his house calls on patients so that we and neighbors could ride with him to high school. Dad also helped Ernie with his job of delivering the weekly magazine *Oak Leaves.* When the weather was bad, we could always count on Dad for an assist.

In high school days, Ernie would sometimes have good friends over to our house for boxing sessions. Dad had given Ernie a set of brown leather boxing gloves one Christmas, and Ernie would often spar with friends, or, as I said, in front of the full-length mirror on the first landing of our living room staircase.

The sparring with friends was all in good humor. I never saw anyone knocked out—though once, roaring with laughter, they made a mock grave for Al Dungan.

These boxing sessions were always held when our parents were not at home. I was allowed to watch from the balcony at the south end of the music room only because I could keep secrets and would help get the room back in order when the fun was over. I loved being trusted as a kid sister.

In addition to allowing me to watch him box, Ernie always invited me to watch him perform in his swimming meets or football games at Oak Park High School. He considered me his sport-loving sister. I, by the same token, never hesitated to ask him to watch me perform in my sports activities at Holmes

School, where among other things I played softball. Ernie's short story, "Soldier's Home," telling of one Helen playing baseball, could only be about me, the kid sister who adored her big brother and was proud of his returning the affection.

Ernie excelled at swimming more than at football. But Dad liked to see him play football and often went to his games, though he was always fearful of Ernie's getting badly hurt. Personally, I never liked the game; it was too rough, and, as they seemed intent on hiding the football from each other, they indeed hid it from me as well. To this day baseball is my love.

Mother, Dad, and we four children returning from Windemere–1909.

Right: A page from Mama's record, with photo of "us five" ready to return to school. In this book Mama wrote of me: "She is sometimes caught in innocent mischief and sent to the principal's office . . . but she will not tell on her friends, or get them into trouble. She is quite athletic, a good fellow among the boys and girls, at baseball, basketball, volley and indoor ball. She is game–and to be relied on in an emergency. As genuine a boy as ever inhabited a girl's personality . . . she loves to clean fish and chickens, has no squirms like the other girls. The most unusual and interesting child of them all."

Oct 1. 1914
Marcelline
16 yrs 9 mo
140 lbs 5 ft +
8½ in tall
Sophomore
in High School
Ernest
15 yrs 2 mo
140 lbs 5 ft 10½
Sophomore
in High School
Plays on Foot
ball team

Ursula 12 yrs 5 mos - 7th Grade Holmes School —
just returned from Nantucket.
Sunny 9 yrs 10 mo old. 5th Grade. A good
base ball player.   Carol 3 yrs 2 mo old.

Sept 15th 1913

Sunny at 8 yrs 10 mo. old began piano
lessons. She was able to play about 20 pieces
and duets before she ever took a lesson
just from watching her sister Ursula
practice   Her teacher Miss Helen Kennedy
says she has unusual ability and she
loves to practice incessantly.

By June 1914 she has had 30 lessons
has played at 3 recitals and has out-
stripped both her older sisters, who have
studied piano with several teachers
for 5 or 6 years.   When we went away
for the summer Sunny was told she
need not practice during the summer
for fear of falling into bad habits,
but she could not keep away from
the piano, and spent about 3 hours

Left: Carol, Sunny,
Ursula, Ernie, and
Marce–1915.

Bottom left: "We six"
in Oak Park.

Bottom right: Dad
and "Mother Gracie"
in the back yard at
Oak Park.

Facing page, top: Sunny's winning sixth-grade baseball team, with teacher Miss Latus. Sunny, standing to the right, holds sister Carol by the hand.

Bottom: On the lawn at Kenilworth Avenue, Oak Park. The first photo of Mother and her six children– 1915.

Mother with her six children–July 1915.

Ernest Miller Hemingway–June 1916.

ERNEST HEMINGWAY

Class Prophet; Orchestra (1) (2) (3); Trapeze Staff (3), Editor (4); Class Play; Burke Club (3) (4); Athletic Association (1) (2) (4); Boys' High School Club (3) (4); Hanna Club (1) (3) (4); Boys' Rifle Club (1) (2) (3); Major Football (4); Minor Football (2) (3); Track Manager (4); Swimming (4).

"None are to be found more clever than Ernie."

ILLINOIS

MARCELLINE HEMINGWAY

Commencement Speaker; Orchestra (1) (2) (3) (4); Glee Club (3) (4); Tabula Board (4); Trapeze Staff (3), Editor (4); Opera (1) (2) (3); Atalanta (1) (2) (3) (4); Girls' Rifle Club (2) (3) (4); Commercial Club (4); Drama Club (3) (4); Girls' Club (3), Council (4); Story Club (3).

"I'd give a dollar for one of your dimples, Marc."

OBERLIN

Left: Sunny's home run in the fifth grade. Ernest wrote about seeing "Helen" play baseball in a short story.

Below: Daddy, Carol, Mother, Ernie, Les, Ursula, Sunny, and Marcelline–1916.

Facing page, top: Ernest (second from left) with the Oak Park High School swimming team.

Bottom: A page from the Oak Park and River Forest Township High School "Senior Tabula" showing Ernie–the "Class Prophet"–and Marce. Both Ernie and Marce were involved in a good many class activities.

Right: A note from Sunny: "Dear Neighbors: I am sorry to relate to you that your nice kitty has been very brutal while you left her outdoors with no food but to live on our baby chickens. I did not do anything to her because it wasn't her fault. She had to have something to eat. I hope you will see this stops because we don't raise chickens for cats to eat. Yours truly, Sunny Hemingway. P.S.: 2 chickens eaten."

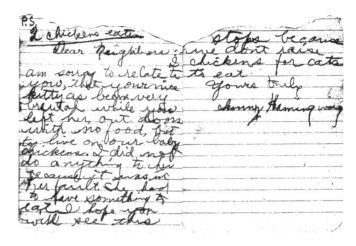

Above left: Ernie in the back yard of the Kenilworth Avenue house.

Above right: Ernie and Marce in Oak Park.

Right: Ernie and Daddy.

Facing page, top left: Decoration Day, 1916: All of us, except Daddy.

Facing page, top right: Mother with her six children, Sunny fondly leaning on Ernest.

Facing page, bottom: "Our family" in Oak Park.

Right: Ernest's high school teacher, Miss Fanny Biggs, entertained at our home, along with Ernie's friend, Clarence Savage. Miss Biggs was one of the first to recognize Ernest's talent and encourage him to write.

Below: A page from the program for the Oak Park and River Forest Township High School class play. The cast included Ernest Hemingway playing Richard Brinsley Sheridan.

"BEAU BRUMMEL"
By Clyde Fitch

given under the management of the

ENGLISH DEPARTMENT

of the

Oak Park and River Forest Township High School

Dramatic Director	. . . .	Miss Margaret H. Dixon
Stage Director	. . . .	Miss Essie Chamberlain
Musical Director	. . . .	Mr. O. Gordon Erickson
Director of Dances	. . .	Miss Marjorie H. Hull
Business Managers	. . .	{ Mr. Everett M. Owen
		Mr. Frank J. Platt

High School Auditorium, Oak Park, Illinois

FRIDAY, FEBRUARY 16, 1917, at 8 P. M.

Class Play Cast

Beau Brummel	Morris Musselman
The Prince of Wales	Thomas Cusack
Richard Brinsley Sheridan	Ernest Hemingway
Lord Manly	Robert Cole
Reginald Courtenay	Dale Bumstead
Mortimer	Le Roy Huxham
Mr. Abrahams	Allen Speelman
Simpson	Julian Lull
Bailiffs	Harry King, Lyman Worthington
Prince's Footman	Ray Ohlsen
Mr. Oliver Vincent	Lloyd Golder
Mariana Vincent	Dorothy Estabrook
Kathleen	Gladys Johnson
The Duchess of Leamington	Elizabeth Wanzer
Lady Farthingale	Carroll Dyrenforth
French Lodging House Keeper	Olga Flohr
Mrs. St. Aubyn	Roberta Finnell

Other Ladies and Gentlemen

Betty Bryden	Hilyard Gage
Ruth Morrison	Franklin Lee
Helen Shepherd	Paul Porch
Carolyn Bagley	

Program

---

1. **The President's Speech**
   "Doing Our Bit"
   Robert Mason Cole

2. **Class Oration**
   "Dreamers as World Builders"
   LeRoy Edward Huxham

3. **Class Poem**
   Virginia Dorsett Reid

4. **Class History**
   Esther Mary Pomeroy

5. **Class Prophecy**
   Ernest Miller Hemingway

6. **The Ax**
   Fred Stewart Wilcoxen, Jr.

7. **Class Gift**
   Dorothy Louise Estabrook

Senior Stunt

The Gringola

Participants

Edward Wilson	Harry King
Lyman Worthington	Morris Musselman
Chester Clifford	Joel Crissey
Henry Bredfield	Hale Printup
Richard Bredfield	Arthur Thexton
	Gertrude Early

...age from Ernie's graduation program and senior class photo. Ernest is second from right in front row, and Marce is ...d from left in second row.

22
Uncle Tyley

Mother's uncle, Benjamin Tyley Hancock, a descendant of John Hancock, whom we all called Uncle Tyley, lived with us for years. He was a traveling salesman when he was younger, and whenever he came to the Chicago area, his room was ready for him on the third floor of the Oak Park house.

After dinner Uncle Tyley would go to his room to smoke his pipe and fiddle a little on his violin. It was a treat to be allowed to go to his room and listen to his tales of adventure on his travels.

He sometimes took Ursula and me walking in the new-fallen sparkling snow at night, just when the street lights came on. He put magic in the simplest exploits.

For the children of our family, Uncle Tyley could do no wrong. His playtime with us before dinner was enhanced by his sometimes pretending to find a penny behind our ears. His sleight of hand demonstrations endeared him to all of us at one age or another. He was our wonderful bachelor uncle, Grandmother Hall's brother.

He was an excellent domino and checker player, and we enjoyed his companionship for many years before he went out to Santa Barbara to live, and later die of old age with the Clarence Roomes, my mother's relatives. When he died, he was brought back to Oak Park and a graveside service was held at Forest Home Cemetery in Forest Park, Illinois, where most of our parents' relatives are buried, and our immediate kinfolk.

In many of Ernest's letters home, he would send "love to Uncle Tyley."

I imagine now that Ernest knew the truth about when Uncle Tyley would have someone call my father to come and get him at one of the Forest Park

"We caught it! Didn't we?"
Ursula and her Grand-Uncle
Tyley.

saloons, such as Otto's. I never knew until years later that he was drunk on those occasions. Daddy always told us that Uncle was sick and should not be disturbed for a day or two. When Prohibition came, there was a distinct change in Uncle Tyley. A law-abiding citizen—as I heard it later—he never took another drop of alcohol from that day on.

He lived to a fine old age of ninety or so. We believe he was partially preserved in alcohol.

23
The War

Early in 1918, after spending six months in Kansas City as a reporter for the *Kansas City Star,* Ernie went away to the war. He had not been gone three months when he was badly wounded on the Italian front. He had volunteered to go to the front, his friend Ted Brumback advised Dad in a letter of July 14, thinking he "could do more good and be of more service by going straight up to the trenches."

Ted—or "Brummy" as Ernest often called him—wrote Dad the July 14 letter from the American Red Cross hospital in Milan soon after Ernest was wounded. He reported that Ernie had been on the Piave front helping the Italians in the front lines when a trench mortar exploded, killing one Italian and seriously wounding Ernest and two other Italian soldiers. Though badly hurt himself, Ernest had carried one of the wounded Italian soldiers on his back to the first aid section. Ernest had been treated at the front and then sent to the Red Cross hospital in Milan with "some two hundred pieces of shell . . . lodged in him." But Ernie was recovering and would not have any trouble about most of the wounds.

Dad could be "very proud" of Ernest, the letter said. He would receive a "silver medal of valor which is a very high medal indeed and corresponds to the Medaille Militaire or Legion of Honor of France."

Ernie, unable to write much himself because of shell splinters in his fingers, added a postscript to Ted's letter saying that he was okay and sending love to our parents. He was not near so much of a "hell roarer" as Brummy made him out, he said.

Dad also received a letter from the American Red Cross in Washington. Ernest would be receiving the "Italian Cross of War" for his work on the Piave.

Above: Two photos of Ernie in Italy.

Left: Lieut. Ernest M. Hemingway–
1918.

A page from the October 5, 1918, issue of "Oak Leaves" with a story on Ernie. They printed his letter to us from Italy talking about his wounds.

"During every minute of [the] attack," the letter said, "the men worked night and day under fire, performing service of the highest importance .... [Ernest] was wounded by a bomb from a trench mortar and received 237 separate wounds in the legs. All but ten of these wounds are superficial."

Like Ted Brumback, the Red Cross officer felt that Dad must be "very proud indeed of your son and the splendid work which he is doing in helping the Italian soldiers."

Dad—and Mother—were proud of Ernie. They reported the news of his wounding to the Oak Park weekly, *Oak Leaves*, which published a story on Ernie and later even published some of his letters home.

Saturday, October 5, 1918

WOUNDED 227 TIMES

Ernest M. Hemingway Describes His Emotions at Supreme Moment— Letter from American Consul

Dr. C. E. Hemingway, whose son, Ernest M. Hemingway, was the hero of a fine Red Cross exploit in Italy, as told in a recent issue of Oak Leaves, has received a letter from North Winship, American consul at Milan, Italy, praising the courage of the doctor's son and announcing his intention of keeping an eye on him. And from Ernest, in the hospital, comes the following letter:

Dear Folks: Gee, Family, but there must have been a great bubble about my getting shot up. Oak Leaves and the opposition came today and I have begun to think, Family, that maybe you didn't appreciate me when I used to reside in the bosom. It's the next best thing to getting killed and reading your own obituary.

You know they say there isn't anything funny about this war, and there isn't. I wouldn't say

HEMINGWAY IN THE HOSPITAL
Photo of Oak Park boy recovering from wounds in Italian refuge. He is shown whistling, as in his childhood days he would whistle instead of cry, when hurt. This is the first fotograph of local men in an army hospital published in Oak Leaves.

that it was hell, because that's been a bit overworked since General Sherman's time, but there have been about eight times when I would have welcomed hell, just on a chance that it couldn't come up to the phase of war I was experiencing.

For example, in the trenches, during an attack, when a shell makes a direct hit in a group where you're standing. Shells aren't bad except direct hits; you just take chances on the fragments of the bursts. But when there is a direct hit, your pals get spattered all over you; spattered is literal.

During the six days I was up in the front line trenches only fifty yards from the Austrians I got the "rep" of having a charmed life. The "rep" of having one doesn't mean much, but having one does. I hope I have one. That knocking sound is my knuckles striking the wooden bed-tray.

Well I can now hold up my hand and say that I've been shelled by high explosives, shrapnel and gas; shot at by trench mortars, snipers and machine guns, and, as an added attraction, an aeroplane machine gunning the line. I've never had a hand grenade thrown at me, but a rifle grenade struck rather close. Maybe I'll get a hand grenade later.

Now out of all that mess to only get struck by a trench mortar and a machine gun bullet while advancing toward the rear, as the Irish say, was fairly lucky. What, Family?

The 227 wounds I got from the trench mortar didn't hurt a bit at the time, only my feet felt like I had rubber boots full of water on (hot water), and my knee cap was acting queer. The machine gun bullet just felt like a sharp smack on the leg with an icy snow ball. However it spilled me. But I got up again and got my wounded into the dugout. I kind of collapsed at the dugout.

The Italian I had with me had bled all over me and my coat and pants looked like someone had made currant jelly in them and then punched holes to let the pulp out. Well, my captain who was a great pal of mine (it was his dugout) said, "Poor Hem., he'll be R. I. P. soon." Rest in peace, that is.

On August 4 Ernie wrote a letter himself from the Milan hospital. He had no news, he said, because he was still in bed with his legs splinted. The doctor expected to operate on his knee and right foot in several weeks. But he had been taken to a parade the Sunday before, where he had reviewed the troops from the plaza and had been cheered by the crowd and covered with flowers. The girls there had all taken his name to write to him. He had repeatedly taken his cap off to the crowd, he said, and had been thrilled by his reception, though he hadn't acted so.

Ernie was pleased that he had been recommended for both the medal of valor and the silver medal, the second highest decoration possible in Italy. He wrote that the silver medal was similar to England's Victoria Cross.

But he missed home, too. He said he wished he were up fishing at Horton's Bay. The trout could be thankful for the war! But he expected to get them the

A page from an Oak Park paper with a story on Ernie. He had spoken at his old high school about his war experiences.

HEMINGWAY SPEAKS TO HIGH SCHOOL

With Italian Ambulance Service of Red Cross—Later Commissioned in Italian Army

WOUNDED IN PUSH ON PIAVE

By Edwin Wells

Lieut. Ernest M. Hemingway '17, late of the Italian Ambulance Service of the American Red Cross and then of the Italian Army spoke of his experiences in Italy at assembly last Friday. Caroline Bagley a classmate of the speaker introduced him to an audunce the greater part of which already knew him.

"Stein" as he has been nicknamed, had lost none of the manner of speech which made his Ring Lardner letters for the Trapeze of several years ago so interesting. He told of his experiences first in a quiet sector in the Lower Piave and last in the final big Italian drive.

The "Arditi"

He seemed especially interested in a division of the Italian Army called 'Arditi'. "These men" he said, "had been confined in the Italian penal institutions, having committed some slight mistake such as - -well- -murder or arson, and were released on the condition that they would serve in this division which was used by the government for shock troops.

Armed only with revolvers, hand grenades and two bladed short

ERNEST HEMINGWAY

DRAMA CLUB SHOW WILL BE GIVEN MAY 16

By Geraldine Barry

At the Drama Club meeting Tuesday afternoon, it was decided that the club would give its annual show on May 16. The play or plays to be given at this time have not yet been chosen.

There is to be a contest in the

next summer. He also asked Mother to send him a copy of *Oak Leaves* every week.

At home, we all eagerly awaited any news of Ernie. We were delighted to hear from him, or from his friends. On December 13 that year, Ted Brumback wrote again about Ernie. He had hoped to come to Oak Park on his way home, he wrote Mother, to "tell you all about Ernest," but the Red Cross had "arranged about [his] transportation home by way of St. Louis."

Ted had seen Ernest just before leaving Milan, when Ernie was in "rather run down condition":

> He had just recovered from the jaundice. His sickness was due to a perfectly natural, hut rather foolhardy desire to visit the front and see all his friends at work. How he prevailed on the doctor to let him come out there I don't know. But at any rate he arrived when the Italian offensive was at its full height. The excitement and the strain were too much for him in his run down condition.

But Ernest's wounds were all healed, Ted wrote, and except for a limp that he might have for a while, Ernest would probably have "the normal use of his

Ernie and Lieutenant Lore in Europe.

leg." Ted was sorry that Mother would not be seeing her "wonderful son" for a while yet, but Ernest had decided to remain in Italy until he was perfectly well again—not relishing "lying around with nothing to do" in Ernie's words—and Ted felt his decision was wise.

Sending his love to "Doctor Hemingway," Ted repeated that Dad had "a son the Red Cross is proud to speak of." He told Mother to write him if she had any questions about Ernest. Meanwhile, Ted wrote, "several of the Chicago boys who were in the same section with Ernest have promised to come out and see you."

Though disappointed at not meeting Ted and concerned about Ernie's health, Mother was happy to have the letter.

Left: Ernest wheel by friend in Italy. He brought home the hand-knitted robe shown in the photo.

Right: Ernest in the Ambulance Service, Milan, Italy.

24
Ernie Returns

We all rejoiced when Ernie came home from the war in Italy in 1919. He brought us each fine gifts—for Ursula and me, necklaces of silver, bought on the Ponte Vecchio in Florence.

Though shy about his heroism, he relished the attention all of the family gave him and proudly showed us his mementos. When I invited my neighborhood friends over to see our hero, he tolerated the adoration my young friends openly showed him, and even showed off his star shell pistol in our backyard. It was very exciting to all of us. Ernie seemed to enjoy the importance—and certainly deserved and handled it well.

When he returned, I was only fourteen years old. On his first day home, he invited me to his third floor bedroom at our home on Kenilworth Avenue. I was honored and took the steps two by two to have a quiet time with my hero brother just returned from World War I.

"Sit down, Nunbones," he said.

There was no place to sit but the side of the bed facing him. He was sitting in the only chair.

Wow! I wanted to ask him the details of his front line experiences. I wanted to hear about everything that had happened to him that he had done since he left home. But the first thing I blurted out got squelched.

"Don't ask me about that, Nunbones, and don't ask to see my pictures yet," he said. "I'll tell you anything later, but right now let's have a drink."

Then he poured me a strange liqueur that was really very potent to me, and he handed me a cigar.

"Smoke that, kid, and we'll be friends again."

Of course I smoked, and I drank what he gave me, and I managed to keep a hold on myself so as not to fall flat on my face. I was always honored to be invited to talk to him privately.

Before he'd gone away, it had been a joy to joke and converse with him while he shaved. He'd told me I was the only one he'd ever allow to watch him shave. That had started our private talks together and contributed to our creating a secret language. We had original, seemingly meaningless words for many things and people, so we could talk right in front of our family and not be understood. They considered it a joke, but we considered it powerful. I try now to remember some of it. Once in a while a word will creep out of my subconscious, but it's really gone. My brother Les suggested I go to a good hypnotist and have him try to release the forgotten language, but I can see no point in that. There's no way to prove or disprove the results now that Ernest is not living, and the language only had meaning to us.

Ernie taught me beautiful swear words and phrases in Italian from the war. When we were with his friends, he would get me to swear for them and show me off. He taught me a really dirty song that they sang in Italy, and that, too, though I knew only a portion of its translation, I sang on call—with gusto. But never for any members of our family!

In our family, if any of us spoke a vulgar or questionable word, or worse, a group of words, we used to be ordered to go and wash our mouths out with soap. As children, Ernie and I had been the worst offenders. So we'd kept a bar of Jap Rose soap handy. If you recall, Jap Rose soap was a transparent soap, beautifully scented for fragrance and taste.

After a Jap Rose soaping, we'd return to the fold, and when questioned as to whether we had completed the order, we'd say yes with pleasure. When

Bill Smith, Charles ("Hop Head") Hopkins, and Ernie "horsing around for the picture." Ernie is wearing the Arditi red cap he brought home from Italy.

Dad had taken time to see the task done himself, however, it had been a different, foamy, disagreeable experience.

Once when we were watching some children playing in our back yard, I remarked spontaneously, "Isn't Carol a cute little bugger?"

"Don't ever say that, Nunbones!" Ernie loudly commanded. "That's a dirty word. Never! Promise me never to say that again without my permission. Promise?"

I promised, as he had hold of my arm firmly. And I have never said it yet, as there never was permission given.

It took me years to find out what a "bugger" was. Dad had told Ernie, but Ernie never told me. I still think it a cute-sounding word.

"We six" after the war, at 600 North Kenilworth Avenue.

25
Setting the Record Straight

So often when one member of a family becomes world famous, as our Ernest has, the sensational bits of news, characteristics, and happenings of all the family are grossly exaggerated. It is quite a pain to read in detailed accounts—written for profit or spite—characteristics of our family that are so far from the truth.

One motion picture that comprised the essence of Ernie's short stories, and represented itself as depicting the real life of Ernest, really gave the moviegoing public a very false picture of our family. The movie showed Mother as a thin, heartless, religious fanatic, having no understanding. And it portrayed Ernest as returning from the war to find that his father had died.

In reality, Mother Gracie was a formidable, statuesque, talented, gracious woman—greatly admired for her music and paintings, and later for her lecturing and teaching ability. She inspired many people to use their inborn talents to the fullest. And Dad was not a selfish, cheating man with a weak character, as he was portrayed. He was a generous, God-fearing, kindly, gentle man, whom anyone would be honored to call his friend. He lived his Christian life openly and, until he became sick with diabetes and a heart condition, was an example of vigor and manly grace. And he didn't die until 1928, long after Ernie had returned from the war.

It is true that we were a religious family. We always said the blessing before meals. We had morning family prayers, accompanied by a Bible reading and the singing of a hymn or two. It only took a very few minutes. And often during the prayer, Dad would thank the Lord for the good letter from Uncle Bill and Aunt Mary, and after prayers we would all ask to hear the news from them in China.

Because we, the children, were each exposed at an early age to music, Ursula and I were encouraged to learn new hymn tunes on the piano for morning prayers. To be able to play a tune acceptably, we were given fifty cents as an inducement. When it became too easy for me to perform, the fifty cent bonus was reduced to twenty-five, and then eliminated, so only the honor remained.

Our family expected to go to church each Sunday. Churchgoing was never a matter of convenience, or something we did if nothing else was planned. We expected to go and went unless there was a very good reason to be excused.

Mother organized a thirty-voice young people's vested choir at the Third Congregational Church located at Augusta Street and Forest Avenue in Oak Park. We all took part in that, and each of the members was chosen at some time to solo or be part of a duet or quartet. Ernest and Marcelline were part of the older group, and they had many good friends in the choir. We were not compelled to take part in the choir, but we enjoyed it.

Photo of Ernest, thirteen years old, as a choirboy.

Ernest Miller Hemingway–about ten years old–taken by Albert Roose, a visitor to Windemere.

I can't remember being forced to practice the piano, or the other children being forced to practice their chosen instruments. Of course we were encouraged to do so. Ernie later—as a joke answer to the "What contributed to your success?" question—would reply, "I owe it all to the idle hours I spent in the music room playing 'Pop Goes the Weasel' on my cello."

Some of us took to music and, even though not technically perfect or near perfect, made music a joy in our lives. I can still hear Leicester sawing away on his violin McDowell's beautiful "To a Wild Rose." Some children lost interest entirely and went on to other art forms. But we were each taken to the Grand Opera and symphony concerts in Chicago, and later the Art Institute, as special treats.

Our parents tried to give us each an appreciation of the arts. Dad read aloud to us from Dickens and magazines such as *St. Nicholas* and *Youth's Companion*. We all looked forward to such evenings as a family group sitting around the fireplace. Of course, with such a variety of temperaments, there were some healthy arguments and verbal wars. Ernest had the habit of pointing his third finger at an accused, saying, for instance, "Who hid my hat?" Soon his hat was found behind a radiator—where he'd tossed it.

Because Mother excelled in singing, she tried to develop that ability in each child. Marcelline was the only one of the six who got very far in that line. Mother really saw hopes for Marcelline's voice, but Marce's interest changed to drama before she sang very much publicly. Ernest tolerated the experiment of cultivating his voice for a while, and later his cello playing. He played in the Oak Park High School orchestra. Ursula lost the ability to find middle C, she said, and after the allotted time of study at the piano changed her interest to Saturday afternoon classes at the Art Institute. Later she excelled in ceramics and flower growing. Carol, the darling of the other children, seemed to have the least interest in music, but her writing and academic abilities were great. It's odd that the most scatterbrained of the six children—I, Sunny, the fourthborn, who learned to prefer the neck of the chicken—should still have music such a big part of my life. I even played the harp in the Memphis Symphony Orchestra. I would rather be without a stove than a piano or organ. Leicester was a good student and has excelled in writing. Having so famous a brother has been both an advantage and a disadvantage to him.

◆ ◆ ◆

I have read that Ernie ran away from home. Our parents always knew where he was and helped him plan and pack for his trips. And he always sent back the self-addressed postcards Dad gave him on departure with interesting news of his exploits and whereabouts.

He wrote, too, telling us his plans. When he was in Kansas City working for the *Kansas City Star,* where he'd gone right after leaving high school in 1917, Ernie wrote Dad from the Hotel Muehlebach. He impressed upon Dad that although under twenty, he had been working exceptionally hard and was competing with far older men of far more experience. He said, however, that he was doing well, getting good assignments. But he was considering leaving the *Star* and going to Dallas or Topeka, or perhaps St. Louis, where he could earn higher pay.

Ernie complained in the letter that he was tired from all the hard work and took some pains to point out to Dad how much responsibility rested on him as a newspaperman, even adding a piece at the end of his letter describing in detail the difficulty of writing to meet a deadline. Everything, he said, had to be done in a hurry, and yet a reporter had to be absolutely perfect in his style and in his facts.

Because of all the hard work, Ernie said, he badly needed a vacation and intended to take a fishing trip to give his thoroughly exhausted brain a rest. He expected that after his vacation, he would decide whether or not to return to the *Star.* Meanwhile, he also had other prospects. He would see us, he said, in Oak Park in May.

Another letter we saved was one Ernie wrote Dad and Mother from the office of the *Toronto Star* after his arrival there in January 1920, as a single man. He first explained why they had not heard from him for a while; he had written, but had not mailed the letters. This letter, he said, he would try to mail.

He had not caught the mumps, he reported, though young Ralph Connable had had a bad case. He had been playing tennis a good deal. And he had made a trip to Buffalo, where he had seen an old Italian buddy, Arthur Thomson.

He was very pleased about his work on the *Star*. One piece he'd written, he said, had been quoted in a *Globe* editorial, and the owner of the *Star* had spoken favorably to him about it.

He wrote that he was planning to be in Chicago in several weeks before driving up north with Bill Smith. He would stop with us for several days. He intended to write some stories on the outdoors for the *Star* while up north; the *Star* people thought him an expert on camping and trout fishing. He used people like Bill Smith and Jack Pentecost in his stories, he said, and his boss didn't know who they were.

Ernie closed his letter with love, as always.

◆ ◆ ◆

Anyone who had always been close to the activities of my brother in our growing-up days, as I was, would certainly grieve and remember such an emotional upheaval as a runaway episode would inspire. I have no such memory. I remember well when Sister Marcelline, upon being thwarted in some desire, disappeared. My father and I traced her and brought her home promptly, from friends on the South Side of Chicago.

If a fellow wants to amuse a dull audience, he sometimes fabricates happenings to liven up the moment. Ernie always had that ability. But anything uttered became authentic—without reservation—to listeners guilty of wining and dining on and on for ulterior motives.

I have no doubt that one recorded voice of Ernest was made under alcoholic influence and unreasonable encouragement. That will suffice as an example of people who will go to any length to make money on the name of Hemingway. I had been warned not to listen to that recording, but when the record was presented to me I weakened, and in dead quiet and privacy, I heard the voice of my beloved brother. I was shocked and deeply hurt. And yet morbidly I listened to every word. I am still trying to forgive the perpetrators of such a vile display of disloyalty.

It was always hard for Ernie to refuse a request. Many students sent manuscripts to him to criticize or evaluate, and he tried to be helpful when he could. That fine trait he inherited from our father. Dad did more missionary work in his medical practice than people will ever know. It was a family joke that when he announced he was about to take a good, long, hot bath after a long day's work, we could expect an emergency to send him out immediately.

Dad was always on call, in any weather or circumstances. I remember when we would be planning to take the train or Lake Michigan boat for our

Ernest, with a friend, playing "ambulance driver" on Les's toy auto after World War I.

summer vacations, Dad would plan to leave the house at least an hour earlier than necessary so that if he was called unexpectedly, we would still get on our way.

After Dad's death, a feeble effort was made to collect outstanding bills that showed up. A few good patients volunteered the money they knew they owed him but had not yet been billed for. Dad's system of bookkeeping was unique. Many patients never were billed because he felt it would be a hardship to them. He would say that if they could pay, they would, because they appreciated all he had done for them. His fees were small, but his services huge. Night and day he was on call.

I have read little about the genuine concern and great generosity of my brother Ernest. He was always willing to lend money, and also to give. I know of one instance when he was called upon, by a pleading letter, to save a friend of our parents from disaster. Although he didn't have the needed amount at the time, his credit was good, so he borrowed it. He was never paid back, so of course he took the loss, without thanks.

When my husband, Kenneth Sinclair Mainland, dropped dead without any warning, I sent word to my brothers and sisters, stating the solemn facts. Ernie, in Cuba, tried over and over to break through the telephone system. He had to settle for sending a cable instead, and followed it with a letter of detailed questions to see what we needed to tide us over until the insurance claims could be settled. He didn't know what to advise me about selling the house, worrying that any lump sum of money might run out, leaving me with nothing at all. He did advise me to get insurance and keep some savings against an emergency. Always sensitive, Ernie apologized for writing so businesslike a letter, but he understood that there really wasn't anything that could be said to compensate for the loss of a beloved mate.

Ernest, like me, boasted to gullible people about our Indian blood. That was untrue. Because our father had been on a summer survey trip with some Indians during his Oberlin College days and had told us many tales of his exploits, we enjoyed telling about Dad's Indian name. Those Indian friends that summer had named him "Ne-teck-ta-la," meaning "Eagle Eye." Dad had keen, piercing eyes that looked right through you when he was serious.

At an early age, I really thought I was part Indian and boasted of it to my friends until Mother set me straight emphatically.

I wish Mother were here now to set a lot of people straight on the many untruths and exaggerations that have been written regarding members of our family. But the many family pictures that Mother kept for each of the children in the baby books refute the idea that got started about Mother dressing Ernest as a girl, and that he and Marcelline were dressed as twins. Sometimes we dressed up for Dad's picture taking sessions, or acted pretty silly. When Ernie was home from the war, for instance, he posed on Les's toy auto. We weren't posing for posterity in those days. No one knew that in later years, because of Ernest's success and ability as a writer, every detail of our lives would be interpreted by others.

Take anyone's family—yours, maybe—and see how it would look to the public in unadulterated detail.

The collecting of data and remembrances is a precious responsibility that I take seriously.

26
Hadley

It seemed a royal gyp to me not to be able to attend Ernie's wedding to Hadley Richardson. I had been sent to a girls' camp at Cass Lake, Minnesota, that summer, and no amount of pleading changed my parents' minds. Because of the conflict in dates, I had to go directly to Grandfather and Grandmother Hemingway's home on Oak Park Avenue.

All our family had a fine regard for Hadley from the first, and this grew to be a lasting love. I got to know Hadley later; we've been friends for many years and still keep in touch.

After the wedding in Horton's Bay, Ernie and Hadley honeymooned at Windemere. Later, our neighbor Earl Bacon drove Ernie and Hadley to Petoskey to catch their train to Chicago. Earl told me that because of bad roads, he drove them on a circuitous route. At the top of the old Washout Road—now Eppler Road— Ernie asked him to stop. They were overlooking Little Traverse Bay.

"See all that," Ernie said to Hadley. "Talk about the beauty of the Bay of Naples! I've seen them both, and no place is more beautiful than Little Traverse in its autumn colors."

Hadley agreed it was exquisite.

Ernie and Hadley wrote frequently to Mother and Dad after they moved to Toronto in the fall of 1923. Ernest's experiences as a correspondent in Europe and his many summers at Walloon Lake were being turned into fiction and he was writing easily and well. But the birth of their first child—John, or Bumby—had complicated their daily living considerably. Hadley was both tired and nervous from the amount of traveling they had just done.

In one letter—written from 1599 Bathurst Street in Toronto on November 4, 1923—Hadley commented in depth about her health, the difficulties

Below: The Methodist church in Horton's Bay where Ernie and Hadley were married on September 3, 1921. Their marriage was registered in the Episcopal church files because an Episcopal minister performed the ceremony.

they were having with John's nurse, and what was going on in their household at that time. She wrote proudly of Ernest's short story "My Old Man" being given the place of honor in Edward O'Brien's *Best Short Stories for 1923*, and that the whole book was dedicated to him! She said that was about the biggest advertisement Ernie could have in the storywriting market. She was also enthusiastic about Boni and Liveright wanting him to write a book for them, which, she said, "we are planning for him to do at the earliest possible moment." She signed the letter with "ever so much love from us all, devotedly your daughter, Hadley."

On the back of that letter, Ernie wrote a brief note to Mother and Dad. He was sorry not to have written sooner, he said, but they were not to worry. His story "My Old Man" had nothing to do "with the paternal"; it was just a

M. E. Ch. Hortons' Bay, Mich.

Ernest Miller Hemingway and Hadley Richardson Hemingway at their wedding.

story of a kid whose father was a jockey. He wrote that the book containing the story would probably be on sale by January of the coming year. Ernie told Mother and Dad that the book they had ordered from Three Mountains Press in Paris was being printed while he was writing to them.

They ought to have it delivered fairly soon. It would be published under the title *In Our Time.*

In this same letter, Ernie said the baby was well but had taken to hollering; doubtless he would be some fun in three or four years. As to future plans, they might be going back to Paris in January. They had been trying to figure out some way they could all come to Oak Park for Christmas as they wanted to see all the family so much. But it looked pretty hopeless, Ernie said, from two standpoints: expense, and making the round trip with a nursing baby.

Soon afterward, Ernie, Hadley, and Bumby did go to Paris. Ernie wrote Mother from there on October 9, 1925, telling her about the Boni and Liveright publication of *In Our Time* and asking if she'd seen that book yet. He thanked her for a check she'd sent for a picture frame, saying that Hadley and he were eagerly awaiting the picture itself. He also reported on Bumby's second birthday.

As usual, he wrote about his plans. He would be going to Schruns in December and might go sailing in the Mediterranean with the Murphys after that. He would be working on his novel, which became *The Sun Also Rises,* down at Schruns since it needed a lot of revision before being sent to his New York publishers.

At Ernie's wedding–1921.

In that letter, Ernie also wrote that he was teaching boxing several times a week. Ivan Apfer, the caricaturist, Nathan Asch, the writer, F. Scott Fitzgerald,

and several painters were among his pupils.

Ernie closed with news that Hadley and Bumby were well, and said that all sent their love.

Ernest and Hadley, and later Pauline, Ernie's second wife, were faithful about writing home to the family. Their news of travel and accomplishments greatly interested everyone. Before Ernie had married, his letters had often been shared with friends and relatives. Now they became, for long periods of time, our only personal link with him. Ernie's life, we knew, was moving rapidly; his experiences and friends were different, and his fame grew year by year. Mother and Dad did not always understand his writing, or some of the decisions he made. But in many ways the family remained close.

One time after her divorce from Ernest in 1927, Hadley brought young Bumby to Oak Park to see us. Bumby couldn't speak much English, and we were unable to speak French, but Daddy took him in his Ford touring car, one of the last Model Ts. While those two were out calling on patients and friends and buying Bumby an air rifle, I took Hadley with me to my golf lesson. We were able to talk frankly.

Ernie's wedding at Horton's Bay. With Ernie and Hadley are Carol, Ursula, Mother, Leicester Clarence, and Dad. I had been sent to camp and missed the "big doings."

Mother and Dad at Ernie's wedding.

She told me that if she'd been smart, she would have encouraged Ernest, at the very first sign of his infatuation, to take Pauline off somewhere and burn out the sex appeal they had for each other.

To me it didn't seem right that Hadley—who had encouraged and inspired Ernie and had lived through all the lean years gracefully—should now not share his growing success. But Pauline, who evidently was determined to break up this fine marriage, took advantage of her chance to win Ernie while her friend Hadley was busy caring for Bumby, who was sick at the time, in a borrowed villa. Ernie was used to admiration and flattery, but the combination of circumstances was too much at that time.

I don't believe Ernie ever felt right about that breakup. It probably made it easier, afterward, for him to make more marital changes.

Years later, when I was in Key West with him and Pauline, and he was getting what he called "fortified"—with drink—to go to his adopted religion's confession, I asked him, if his Catholicism didn't recognize his former marriage, what did that make Bumby? A bastard?

"Certainly not," he said. "We don't go that far."

When Pauline and I got into one of our rare conversational moods, I told her I was in love with a married man but could do nothing about it. She told me to go ahead and get him. She had found who she wanted, she said, and had gotten him, and was glad she had.

I hoped she would get the same treatment.

And she did.

27
A Missed Adventure

Ernie had a running sense of adventure. In the back of his mind, there always seemed to be plans, or information for making plans, for the next trip. Because I had been his kid sister with the greatest liking for boxing, baseball, swimming, hunting, and fishing, he trusted me with some of his private thoughts and with a great many of his reactions to family squabbles.

I trusted him, too, and often went to him when I had an important decision. I had begun to think about what my own life was going to be. Being raised in a doctor's family, and having Uncle Bill a medical missionary in China, I became fascinated with the medical progression. But since I was a poor student, I could not see myself as doctor.

Talking with me one time, after a firm reprimand regarding my report card, Daddy suggested I might make a very good nurse. The thought hit me just right. My two older sisters had switched from one interest to another. Ernest alone, since his high school days, had calmly headed for a writing career.

I finally graduated from Oak Park High School in the mid-year class of '24, and my father, proud of my decision, immediately made plans for me to enter West Suburban Hospital for nurse's training. After two years' training, I thought I was in love with a patient named Robert St. John. I enjoyed our secret meetings and note passing when I was off duty. Bob influenced me to stop nurse's training and try college.

I remember writing Ernie at the time for his opinion of this man. He answered promptly, honored that I had consulted him, and allowed as how any guy who could work as a rewrite man on that particular Chicago newspaper must be a good guy and just might be worthy of his kid sister.

But Bob and I fell out of love as easily as we had fallen in.

My college education was short-lived. After three days in chemistry, I realized I was wasting the professor's time—and mine. Also, chemistry was an eight o'clock class. A few months later I changed to a business school to learn typing and shorthand.

It wasn't long before I got a job in a dentist's office, where I learned about casting inlays, setting up teeth for dentures, sterilizing instruments in a quart-sized machine, and much else.

By the spring of 1927, I was feeling fed up with my work at the dentist's office, and with the dentist himself, who was a severe disciplinarian. Ernie wrote me to write him at his Paris address and tell him whether I wanted to come over for a vacation. He told me to go into my financial situation clearly so he would know how much chance there was of making my old dream come true. No one else in the family had been in Europe with Ernie.

I wrote Ernie that I knew his domestic situation had changed since he'd divorced Hadley and married Pauline. I didn't know exactly how things were with him in Paris, and I didn't want to "horn in." He wrote back with one of the longest handwritten letters I've ever seen. He made me welcome, condemned my thought of possibly "horning in," and proceeded to explain his plans.

I was to address him in care of Guarantee Trust Company of New York, at 1, rue des Italiens, in Paris. He had rented a new apartment since he had written me the first time and there was plenty of room to put me up. He was looking forward to the next two months. The biggest news to me was that he and Pauline had worked together over the wording of a cable they had sent me asking me to come the middle of June and go to Pamplona with Ernie for the fiesta, with all expenses paid. That part was of real importance to me, for it let me know I was equally acceptable as a guest to Pauline, whom I had never seen but about whom I had heard a great deal.

Ernie's letter was as explicit as a will about a number of things. He started out feeling a little hurt that I might have thought he was as close with money as our notoriously nonsplurging parents. He swiftly corrected any such impression I might have, and insisted that all expenses, once I reached Europe, would be on him—that while he had a sou, it would be at my disposal.

This letter, written May 6, urged me to come on over, no matter what discouragement I might get from others around me. Ernie wanted me to come by the first of June, saying that he would personally meet me at the boat train. His plan was for me to be in Paris for a couple of weeks, and, as a starter, for him to show me the city. Then Spain! He explained that Pauline was having a friend, Clara Dunn, come over to France at about the same time for a long visit. Pauline and Clara could pal around together while he and I took off for the week's fiesta in Pamplona.

It would not be good for Pauline to go to Pamplona this year, Ernie felt, as he had been there with Hadley only the year before. I would be a godsend to him if I'd be his traveling companion at the festivities, which started on July 6 and were to be over by the 13th. After the fiesta, I could either go back up to Paris, or join Pauline's sister Virginia and take a trip on the Riviera. He threatened me. I was not to pull any final decision stuff about not being able to come, or he'd be through with me.

Exuberant about the coming adventure, Ernie wrote that in his opinion, this would be the best chance I'd ever have to take a trip with him; I had better tighten up the old belt and come along. He repeated that he would be picking up the tab for everything in Paris and Pamplona—the railroad fare, the bullfight tickets, the wines, beers, cigars, and all else. And he would take care of getting me back to the boat if I were pressed for money in any way. He advised me to sail as a student, third class, to save money on the transatlantic fare. By my coming to Europe now, he went on, he and I would nail any gloating by the family, and I would be the first of all the kids to see Europe with him, and he would have a grand time showing it to me.

In the same letter, Ernie explained that he had turned over to Hadley all the money from the British and American rights of *The Sun Also Rises*, and as a consequence she was in swell financial shape. He was feeling awfully cheerful at his own improved situation, saying he had sold a story to *Atlantic Monthly* for more than three hundred dollars and that he had just sold three stories to *Scribner's*.

Ernie was explicit about my not telling anyone the details he had just written in the first four pages of this letter. He was literally thinking on paper as he wrote, and periodically throughout the letter urged that I drop the noncoming thinking and get on with the actual arrangements to come and enjoy everything that we had in prospect. He knew it was a hardship for the family not to have the inside track on his private life, he added, but they had never merited his confidence, nor backed him, and fond as he was of them, he refused to carry the extra weight of home criticism while getting on with his life.

He would tell the family what was going on in his own good time.

As to Pamplona, Ernie felt I would be crazy about the fiesta there and would be able to see all *The Sun Also Rises* stuff. He was sure I'd like Pauline, and mentioned that I might even still like him. He knew—though I hadn't said so—that I was upset about the breakup with Hadley.

Ernie assured me that my trip would be highly acceptable to the other sisters, and that he loved me, and said that the family wasn't showing proper appreciation of me. With him I would be a royal guest, and I'd have a chance to buy some clothes for myself if I had any dough saved for the trip.

After a few gibes at another member of the family for having inherited the family genius for not being free with funds, Ernie finally reached the end of his marvelous, long letter with one final urging that I come soon, while he was still above the sod. He couldn't guarantee that that would be longer than the summer just ahead, but he was my devoted brother, would see me in June, and wanted me not to let anything on earth change my plans.

With a letter like this, every one of millions of young women— whether kid sisters or not—would have rushed down to the nearest travel agency to inquire about the lowest fare to New York, and how soon all plans could be made. I read this lengthy, sublime invitation over and over in the privacy of my room. I desperately wanted to go.

But then a series of small but upsetting things kept happening, one after the other, and the following month I finally had to decide, with the greatest reluctance, that I simply couldn't make the trip.

I always felt that Ernie never understood my reasons for not following through. When he wanted to do something, he just did it. All his life he remained " 'fraid of nothing." He had had the trip all dreamed up in detail and had counted on me, and I had failed him.

Though he never harped on my disappointing him, later, in Key West, he once said, "You had your big wonderful chance, Kid, remember?"

28
Pauline

Pauline had a difficult part to play in our family. All of us had been fond of Hadley and were upset at Ernest's divorce. But Mother tried very hard to accept the situation and soon took Pauline into her heart. Pauline seemed to have a fine feeling for Mother, and, like Hadley, wrote her often, with great affection.

Right after the birth of her first son, Patrick, in late June 1928, she wrote from her parents' home in Piggott, Arkansas:

> My dear Mother Hemingway:
>
> Well, here we are at last, father, mother and son, home from the hospital and it's certainly pretty fine. Patrick and I expect to be here through August, while Ernest goes on a fishing trip out west with a friend and finishes up his book. I do hope they have a glorious trip, for I don't think Ernest has had much fun for the last month—and the month before that for that matter.

Pauline thanked Mother for "cheering [her] on the last lap," saying that Mother's letter had come "just two days before we set out in the night for the hospital." She also thanked her for the blanket she'd sent the baby.

Pauline and Ernest had heard from Marcelline, who was in Paris; and Pauline wrote that they were sorry not to have been in Paris to "welcome" Marce. But Pauline hoped that Mother would visit Paris when they were back there. They did not plan to visit in Michigan since the baby would be "nothing, or rather something to travel with."

Pauline soon began calling our mother "Mother Grace," which seemed to her "less formal than Mother Hemingway." She wrote on July 24, 1928, that "if your grandchildren are calling you Gracie, surely you won't mind Mother Grace."

They were out west, then, with Bumby, while Patrick remained at home in Arkansas. Ernest had gone bear hunting, while Pauline and Bumby stayed at the ranch. Bumby had become "brown and solid," Pauline wrote, from the outdoors and from horseback riding. They would not be able to visit us in Michigan that year, said Pauline—"fate [had] decreed otherwise"—but they hoped to be able to come some other year.

She and Bumby expected to leave shortly as Bumby had to be taken to New York to be sent home to France for school. Ernest would "stay on awhile to get on with his book."

I was in Bermuda then, with Carol, and Pauline wrote Mother in the letter that Ernest had received my "splendid letter."

29
To Key West, with Ernie

In November of 1928, Ernie wrote me instructions to have the Model A Ford he had left with me in Oak Park serviced to absolute perfection for his trip down to Key West. He invited me to go with him. I was to ditch the dentist job, and so that I could continue to save for the European trip I still hadn't taken, he would give me the same cash I was earning if I would type his manuscript of *A Farewell to Arms* and help Pauline with the baby Patrick.

I was ecstatic.

Before we left home, Mother insisted that Ernie sort his trunk that had been kept in the basement for years. I tagged along with him. He proceeded to throw out all kinds of things I thought I'd like to keep.

I asked him for some of the stuff.

"Help yourself, Nunbones," said Ernie. "You'll only throw it out later."

Some I did, and some I saved. I wish I had saved more.

We drove down to Piggott, Arkansas, where Pauline and Patrick were visiting her parents. I did all or most of the night driving, he the daylight, as Ernie preferred it that way. We had wonderful hours of conversation en route.

I told him that lately Dad had told me he was in financial trouble from Florida real estate investments. I had asked Dad why he didn't ask our rich uncle to help him out. Dad said he had asked him, but had been told, coldly, that he had gotten into it and now he could get himself out of it. Uncle had suggested putting a mortgage on our home.

Ernie was furious. "Someday I'll write a piece about this uncle," he said, "and no amount of missionary work he does will whitewash him." I don't think he ever did.

As we approached the Piggott farm—home of the Pfeiffers— Ernie was very eager. I was apprehensive. I was happy to be on the trip but I wasn't sure

Ernie had consulted Pauline about my coming. As I looked back on it all later, I realized she didn't have the whole picture. Ernie was unconcerned; he was anxious to get there. He said he was like a horse smelling the stable.

We stayed in Piggott a few days, long enough to go sunrise duck hunting. I remember—still with fright—the overloaded, small boat that took us to the blind. Ernie wanted me to have a good time, but I really felt unwanted by Pauline from the moment I entered her life. It didn't help any when I shot a live decoy by mistake.

Anyway I felt wanted by Ernie. He enjoyed having me around. That was the important thing.

Ernie and I had always had a fine understanding of each other, and we shared jokes and jibes that could never be explained. His interest in the experiences I had had while in nurse's training at the West Suburban Hospital in Oak Park were a source of many conversations while we drove to Florida.

After a long, quiet period, Ernie would say, "Tell me again, Nunbones, this time in excruciating detail, the one about finding the patient dead in bed in a five-bed ward when you were on night duty. Details! Every feeling you had, thoughts even . . ."

Ernie thought he might use it in a story sometime.

I complied. He was always, as he said, consciously and unconsciously packing away in his mind many sights, sounds, and thoughts for future use. His mind was at work everywhere, at all times.

One story I did tell Ernie was about the dead baby.

One afternoon, when I was alone on duty on the maternity floor, three visitors came to my desk. They said they had come to see the mother who had recently lost her baby. The doctor had said it would be all right, they said, to bring the embalmed baby to the mother for her to say goodbye. That sounded odd to me, so I told them I would have to telephone the supervisor for permission to do such a thing. The supervisor told me, yes, I could do so, but to screen the patient and hand her the baby, and to let her hold it only a minute or two as there might be complications.

I told the supervisor I was alone on the floor and that I wished someone could be sent to assist. But she said it was all right for me to go ahead, though it would be wise to keep the adult visitors out of the room while I let the mother hold the baby.

Reporting all this to the visitors, I proceeded to screen the patient, explaining to her just what I was going to do. She seemed calm and appreciative. So I went into the hall and took the baby from the black suited man.

The baby, dressed and bundled in a pretty blanket, looked like a darling little doll. I laid it gently in the mother's arms, and stepped back to let her have a last, sad look at her firstborn.

She looked a moment, then screamed at the top of her voice. "She's not dead, she's not dead, she's just sleeping! Help me wake her up!"

She shook the corpse, then hugged her so tightly to her bosom that it took all my strength to pull the baby away.

The visitors, having heard the commotion, left as soon as I delivered the baby back to them.

By now, the other new mothers in the ward, who had up to then been most sympathetic with the woman, especially at nursing times, got very upset. One said the woman was crazy and she refused to stay in the room with her another day.

That was one of the most difficult experiences of my life.

After my story, Ernie said only, "You handled it okay, Nunbones. Do you remember any other choice bits?"

"Well, one thing I am certain of," I said, "I can trace my tendency to claustrophobia to a definite time and place in that hospital."

A male patient I had become fond of died. It was my assignment to make him ready and take him down to the hospital morgue where the bodies were then called for by an undertaker. Our morgue was located in the basement. The small service elevator in that wing barely had room for the cart and me.

Going down, the elevator got stuck between floors, for some unexplained reason. Pushing the red button did nothing for much too long. I waited and wondered what to do. Then, distinctly, I saw a movement under that sheet. I was positive I saw him move.

By the time the elevator was released and we landed on the basement floor, I was a wreck.

I told the man on duty in the morgue, but he just laughed. Ever since then, I've hated to be locked in. I ride in elevators, and I try to ignore this tendency. But I suffer now and then from the experience.

Ernie, sympathetic, changed the subject.

When we left Piggott, the plan was that Ernest and I drive as far as Jacksonville, Florida. Pauline and the baby would meet us there and I'd ride the train with them south to Key West while Ernie drove on alone in the Ford. My remembrance of getting to know Pauline on that trip is rather strange. Because of my inexperience and naivete, I was shocked to hear Pauline accept from a stranger, as we left the dining car, his invitation to have a "nightcap" in the club car. I stayed with the baby Patrick in the drawing room and waited what seemed hours for her to return. I worried about her, but could not leave the baby to see how she was faring with the stranger. She finally appeared. She told me nothing, and I told Ernest nothing about our "get acquainted" evening.

I felt immediately that she had put me on a servant level.

30
"At Home" in Key West

When we arrived in Key West and went to the rented house on South Street, everyone tried to be gay. The house was neat and small, with two bedrooms and a living room-dining room area adjoining the kitchen. A front alcove had an old upright piano that Ernie had spoken to me about when influencing me to come with him to Key West. I can't remember now too many details of this furnished house. It was not impressive. But I will never forget the outside pump that seemed to go wild now and then. Someone would have to go out and tinker with it to quiet it almost nightly. I remember always waiting to see if Pauline or Ernie would go out to quiet it, rather than me, as they were at that end of the house. Many times, unable to wait any longer, I made the trip.

As soon as we arrived at the house, I was instructed in the care and feeding of Patrick. And his bed was put in my bedroom at the opposite end of the house so Ernest and Pauline would be spared any noise or interruptions. The typewriter and table were also in my room. I was to start, as soon as possible, the job of typing the valuable manuscript of A Farewell to Arms.

Ernie would work many hours writing and correcting his manuscript, and then give me more pages to type. He wrote behind his closed door and demanded absolute protection from interruptions. It was hard to do all the baby chores as well as type, so sometimes I got far behind with the manuscript.

What Pauline did, when she was not planning meals with the Negro maid, Olive, I really don't know. I was pleased to be with my adored brother and could never even intimate that I felt put upon by his wife. He adored her, and they were happy together, planning fishing trips and social times with friends.

They introduced a couple of local young men to me so I might have a little social life, too.

One man Ernie wanted me to meet was John Dos Passos. Ernie didn't especially appreciate my men friends. So when he invited Dos Passos down, he built him up to me at every opportunity. I began to look forward to his arrival and had a fine mental picture of him. But when he arrived, I was shocked to see a bald man with nervous, jumpy movements. Ernie had neglected to give me a physical picture of his friend, who was nine years older than I. Of course, I didn't play up to Dos, and Ernie was put out by my lack of interest and apparent rudeness.

The visit turned out well for Dos, though. He met—and later married—a longtime friend of ours, Kate Smith, who had come to Key West also.

Sunny in Key West, 1928.

31
Dad Dies

It was about two weeks after I left home that Dad took his own life. I was desperately upset and haunted by the thought that if I had been around to cheer him when that last depression came, I might have gotten him over that bad time. He'd hated to see me leave, yet was glad for my opportunity.

When the message of Dad's death came to Key West—a shocking phone call—Ernie was en route from New York to Key West by train with Bumby. When he got the news, he immediately left young Bumby in the care of a porter and went directly to Oak Park. Those were upsetting days and nights—the news was so hard to believe. For a few days, in Ernie's absence, Pauline was very kind and considerate of me and I appreciated it. She even called in a doctor to quiet me down, for I was terribly distraught.

When Ernest returned to Key West, he told us the details of the tragedy. Dad had had a long illness of diabetes and heart trouble that he'd kept to himself. That, coupled with his financial stress, in part explained his mental attitude toward living. He had I shot himself in the head with a .32 revolver.

But we talked little about Daddy. It was painful to me.

At evening's end, Ernie said, "I'll probably go the same way."

He was half jesting, half serious. The thought seemed most unlikely. Dad had always told us that only a coward commits suicide. We found, though, that when someone you love commits the act, it's easy to find comforting excuses. And you regard him none the less for it.

A portrait of Dad.

32
Friends-and Accidents

I enjoyed Key West and made some friends there. Pauline, exaggerating a little, wrote Mother at Christmastime, "Sunny . . . is being much feted and has the town by the ears, though her heart is in another state in the union altogether." She thanked Mother in that letter for all the Christmas gifts, saying that Patrick was "practically living in his sweater," though she hadn't used her powder puff yet as there had been "no social occasion worthy of powdering the back—or rather we haven't been going out very much as we are living a quiet life until the book is finished."

But Ernie had many interesting visitors during our stay in Key West. Waldo Peirce came. He'd throw his latest sketches or paintings on the floor, spreading them out so we could all see and admire them. While in Key West, he sketched our black maid, Olive. Waldo was buoyant and vivacious, and when he was in a room the atmosphere was full of him and his enthusiasms.

Waldo said he never allowed any professional barber to trim his hair or beard. I told him that since Grandfather Hemingway had preferred me to do those honors for him in his last sickness, I felt qualified. Grandfather Hemingway had made me feel honored and important when he asked for me; I would feel equally honored and important if Waldo would trust me to do him.

Waldo relented and we decided to use the backyard as the barbershop. A brisk wind was blowing, and I clipped away while Ernie stood around giving instructions—"a little more off here," "a little off there"—laughing and kidding and appreciating the show.

Henry Strater, whom Ernie called Mike, also came down and painted a portrait of my brother. Later Max Perkins came down from Scribner's to call for the finished manuscript. He and Ernie were good friends and enjoyed each other's company. And the risk of mailing the manuscript was eliminated by his coming.

One evening, when conversation lagged for a moment, I told Ernest that my local friend, Archie, had asked me about the scar on my right cheek. He peered at me intently and said he could hardly see it; it mostly showed up clearly in hot weather and bright light. I asked Ernie to give me a good answer for those who asked how I had gotten it. The truth—that when quite young I'd gotten a deep scratch from my mother's brooch—was not a tale.

Without hesitation Ernie replied, "Nunbones, tell them that an infuriated Spaniard slashed you with a razor while making violent love to you."

Words were so easy for him.

Once in Key West, Ernie took five-year-old Bumby and me dove hunting. Pauline called Ernest and Bumby "mighty hunters," writing Mother that they kept us "well supplied with game." We were going along fine until Bumby shouted, "Papa, you shot me!"

Oinbones—my pet name for Ernie—rushed over to see what he meant. Sure enough, a single pellet from Ernie's shotgun had ricocheted and penetrated the little guy's leg—but hardly. There was discussion as to whether we could continue to hunt or whether we should make a big thing of the minor wound and return home. We decided to get some doves. In a short time we had enough for a fine dinner.

Once I had an accident. Ernie had planned a fishing trip for some friends who were visiting in Key West. The plan was for me to drive them down to the dock. But before I left the dock to return to Patrick, sleeping at home, we discovered that something important for the trip had been forgotten. Ernie asked me to rush back to the house for it and get back to the dock as soon as possible. Of course, I was on my way immediately, and made the trip back in record time in his Model A Ford.

Having said goodbye a second time, I headed back to the house, but on the way I noticed a fire engine, its siren screeching, speeding toward a smoky area. I couldn't pass up the chance to see firsthand what was on fire. A cigar factory was ablaze, and to get a good view of it, I turned into a shortcut road. I got just a short peek, then started to head home when a junky car rammed into the side of Ernie's car.

The driver and I had a few words and exchanged names and addresses, and I continued home. I dreaded to tell Ernie and Pauline about the accident, even though it had been no fault of mine.

When I finally told him, he said he admired my driving ability, and it was fine how fast I'd gotten back to the dock with the stuff. But being a celebrity and well known in town, he worried constantly about being sued. "Why the hell couldn't you have kept from being hit by a native?" he asked.

Pauline lashed out at me.

After the episode was settled—for seventy-five dollars—the air started to clear again.

33
Europe-Finally

Plans were finally made for us all to go to Europe. We were to sail in April of 1929. Just before we left, Pauline's Uncle Gus Pfeiffer came down. Friends or relatives never stayed at the house; local small hotels always put them up, and they came to our house for meals, social life, and to make fishing dates. It was a great deal like a club, I thought.

When Uncle Gus was leaving, he handed me a hundred dollar bill "toward my trip to Europe." It was the first hundred dollar bill I'd ever seen, let alone held.

I ran into the other room and asked Ernie what I should do.

"Accept it with grace and dignity," was Ernest's advice. "His giving you a bill like that was like your putting a dollar bill in the collection plate."

We quietly praised Sloan's Liniment, Houbigant, and even Three Flowers, as silent contributors. I understood Uncle Gus was a big stockholder in each of those companies.

Uncle Gus was a great guy. He knew the plan was for me to leave with Pauline, Ernest, Patrick, and Bumby, for my long for trip to Europe. Bumby would be returning to his mother Hadley in Paris after having had a few months with his father.

We left Key West by boat for Havana, spent the night at Obres Mundos Hotel there, and sailed the next day on the S.S. *York* of the North German Line for Europe. It was quite a trip! Sixteen days on the water!

Almost as soon as we were on board, Pauline "took to her bed" and I had the baby bed for Patrick in my stateroom on a lower deck, also shared with Bumby. Somehow after the children were asleep at night, Pauline revived to enjoy life aboard.

When I wanted to get away from the children for a while, I would get the steward to stand guard and let me know if they awakened.

I recall, with pleasure, a few interesting times we had. Ernie was in a gay mood. *A Farewell to Arms* was finished and on its way to being published. There was the traditional captain's party, and sometimes I played dominoes in the lounge with a Frenchman of whom Ernest approved. Ernest's ability to converse with passengers in French, German, and Spanish amazed me. And we enjoyed observing the antics of a man who procured for two very beautiful women.

Ernie thought it best to point out the maneuvers "for my education."

When we put into Vigo, Spain, we were met by many small boats with natives selling their goods. Ernie bought me a beautiful lace mantilla. We had enough time to leave the ship and walk up to the town, where we found a fine place for tiny boiled shrimps and beer. Ernest had tipped my steward heavily so I might leave the children. After so much ocean, we all walked like drunken tourists. The natives gawked at us as we noisily meandered up the middle of the road.

A costume ball on the S.S. York *en route to Europe–1929. She sailed from Havana and was sixteen days on the water. Ernie, with beret and moustache, is in front. Sunny, with hand raised, is behind him.*

When we landed at Le Havre, we said goodbye to our many acquaintances from the ship.

After a night in a Le Havre hotel, we took the train to Paris. Ernie always liked my enthusiasm for each new sight and experience. By now he had taught me to be comfortable around people that drank. Having had no experience with alcohol, and having been taught nothing but the evils of it in our home, it had taken a bit of doing to get me to take even a sip. He had started me on sweet vermouth in Key West. After finding vermouth a pleasure, I'd graduated to apricot brandy and champagne.

Sometimes in Key West, Ernie had absinthe that he filtered with a paper cone into water while reading at the dining table. But he'd told me never to drink absinthe as it was poison. He would tell me what to drink, and how much.

Ernie had a great capacity in those days. He drank heavily but I never once saw him drunk.

I had planned to meet an Oak Park friend, Miriam Rickards, in Paris, and from there to go on our tour together. Ernie found a nice pension for me at Numéro 3, rue de Fleurus.

Ernie was most willing and enjoyed showing me his old haunts. We sat at the outdoor tables at the Dôme and Rotonde, and watched the vast variety of characters nearby. Ernie's keen observation of details was astounding. He seemed to see and understand the meaning of every gesture. Before Miriam arrived, he spent a good many of his days showing me around the galleries and museums. Ernest knew where every famous painting I had yearned to see was located, and he took time to help me enjoy every day. His trained eye opened mine, and he was happy to be my appreciated and inspiring teacher.

I remember some of our early morning walks with Bumby and associate them with different odors. The aproned men sweeping and cleaning their entrances each day, and even sweeping their side of the street, intrigued me. And I enjoyed the sight of people on bicycles carrying their long bread loaves, unwrapped.

In the afternoons, I'd often see middle-aged ladies on their bicycles carrying their choice pastries by a swinging ribbon or tape, perhaps going to tea with a friend. I filled my hours observing and getting the "feel" of Paris, catching some of my brother's great affection for the place.

When our itinerary was completed, Ernie saw Miriam and me off on our Cook's Tour of France, Italy, and Switzerland. He warned us not to get into trouble in Italy, especially, as he had no drag there anymore. In fact, he had been barred from traveling in Italy because of something he had written about Mussolini.

During the war, Ernie had been highly thought of in Italy as the first American wounded there. He'd been decorated with the Silver Valor Medal and even made an honorary cousin of King Alfonso. As such, he'd been allowed free travel in the country. But now all that was changed, decisively.

Ernie's parting words were, "If you get into any trouble, don't give my name."

When we returned to Paris from our tour, Ernie came to us with the accumulated mail, and we talked long and fast of our experiences. He was a good listener.

One day Ernest and Pauline arranged a date for us to go to the horse races at Auteuil. It was a beautiful day to ride along the Champs Elysées to the track outside the city. Miriam and I were told to dress up in our very best outfits. This was not only a horse-showing track, I gathered, but a people-showing track.

How right! The gaudy costumes and strutting folk were as exciting to see as the gorgeous horseflesh.

I was so lucky in my choices in the first four races that Ernie asked me my way of picking the winners.

Certainly I knew nothing of the jockeys or the former records of the horses. But I'd noticed that one or two of the horses, while walking around the circular display area, had relieved themselves of what seemed to be gallons of liquid. I figured they would feel fine after such evacuations and, being that much lighter in weight, would run better.

Ernie roared at my explanation. But he let me pick his next horse.

The famed "beginner's luck" held, luckily, and we came home richer.

◆ ◆ ◆

One afternoon Miriam and I took five-year-old Bumby for a fun time. He was a sharp, animated child, and such fun to be with. He really knew his way around, and he took us—rather than our taking him. I was embarrassed when he stopped at a curb to "wee wee" right out in the open. There was no embarrassment to him. Children there were taught to have no inhibitions about natural functions. He told me everyone did it. On the way home, our taxi driver stopped, released his cost accumulating flag on the meter, and without comment went to a round public urinal at the curb that shielded only from the knees up. The stance was obvious, and the sound distinct.

Such comfort stations for men were everywhere. French women, I observed, were not expected ever to need to urinate.

I dwelt on this subject with Ernie later, and he told me simply that men drank more than women, and that women had larger bladders.

"Trash! Humbug!" said I. "Have you ever made a dedicated survey of

American women's bladders? Do you presume we only *powder* in a powder room?"

◆ ◆ ◆

I was an invited guest at times to his apartment at Numéro 6, rue Férou. With Pauline, I understood, people never "dropped in." But it happened many times that interesting friends of theirs, such as Dorothy Parker, Bob Benchley, and others of equal fascination to me, appeared when I was there.

They showed me the skylight chain that F. Scott Fitzgerald had pulled, mistaking it for the plumbing chain, causing Ernie to get his forehead cut badly by the broken glass. They told me of the frantic time they'd had getting him medical attention at midnight in Paris.

When Miriam and I sailed from Le Havre on the French Line's *De Grasse*, Ernest saw us off, presenting me with a large bottle of my favorite apricot brandy. It was a gay goodbye, not at all sad. And Ernest told me what a joy it had been to have me there. I'd had a few months of education "you don't get in any school," he said.

On the voyage back to New York, we had such fascinating companions as "Sandy" Calder (Alexander to you, maybe). He was in the interesting stage of manipulating brass wire into beautiful shapes with his talented fingers and pliers. I still have a lavaliere type necklace he made for me, with a common stone enshrined in artistically bent wire, that I treasure as a memento of the trip. Sandy loved to dance then, and I was often called on to play his favorite "Chloe" on the piano. He perspired heavily while dancing. Maybe he was sweating out the forthcoming brilliance of his now famous mobiles even then.

When Sandy unexpectedly called on us at Windemere Cottage, he—like many of my friends—was not welcomed by my mother. He was much too modern for our old-fashioned family ways. If Ernie had been home, he would have taken my part and fought for a fair deal for me and my friends. He was always my champion.

34
Ernie's Accident

In late 1930 Ernie was badly hurt in an accident. With Dos Passos and another friend, he had been driving from Yellowstone Park to Billings, Montana, when—blinded by the headlights of an oncoming car—he had swerved off the road, turning his car over. He had broken his right arm. Pauline wrote us from St. Vincent's Hospital in Billings:

> The poor fellow has had a very tough time of it, with pain practically all the time, and sleepless nights. It's been more than four weeks now since he changed his position. He sat up this morning for the first time and will sit up again tomorrow. We may be able to leave a week from today, the 8th, but that isn't certain, as the time has been postponed so many times. The numbness in the elbow and the paralysis of the wrist still persist, but the doctor seems to think these will clear up later. But it will be a long time before the arm will be ready for active service again.

Pauline thanked Mother in that letter for "the picture of Ernest at two and a half years," and promised to send pictures of Bumby and Patrick when she got home again. She said, too, that because of their situation, the "fine family reunion [would not] be able to happen," but that she and Ernest looked forward to having Carol in Key West in the spring. She sent love to Mother, to me, to Ursula, and to "young Hemingway" (Leicester).

Ernie's arm healed slowly, and it was a long time until he was able to write again. He spent the spring in Key West and then made another trip to Spain with Pauline. And in November 1931 we received a happier letter from Pauline. She wrote Mother on November 28 to announce the arrival of her and Ernest's second son, Gregory: "It's just two weeks ago today that Gregory saw daylight and both mother and child are doing very well, tho we shall probably be here several weeks longer to get strong for the long trip to Florida . . . . Gregory is a big healthy strong child, very fond of sleeping and eating. Ernest says he's the handsomest baby he's had yet." Pauline thanked us for all the gifts and good wishes we had sent, and said that now she and Ernest were anxious to get back to Key West, get the house in order, and enjoy Christmas there.

She asked particularly about me. She and Ernest were "distressed over Sunny's stomach back-sliding the way it has." She would write me soon, she said, as my letters were "always so amusing." She had enjoyed the "fine Chinese joke"—which I can't remember—in my last letter.

Ernie and Pauline did get back to Key West for the holiday season, and Carol went down and spent the holidays with them. When Pauline sent a New Year's letter, she reported that Ernest and Carol were off fishing. Pauline was delighted, as usual, with the Christmas gifts, and especially thanked Mother for a pewter dish she had sent for the Key West house.

35
Notes from Their Travels

Ernie and Pauline, of course, traveled a good deal, both in the United States and abroad. The next letter from Pauline I have, written on August 2, 1932, came from the L-T Ranch in Livingston, Montana. Ernie was resting up there, wrote Pauline, after an illness following the "rather hectic time in Florida." They planned to spend the summer at the ranch, and Ernie would stay on to hunt in the fall when Pauline returned to Key West to supervise more renovations on the house. Pauline wrote that Gregory resembled his father at three months—Mother had sent Ernie's baby picture—and was a "darling child . . . very handsome."

Pauline always sounded pleased about her children in her letters to us, though she once wrote Mother, "Aren't you pleased you've so nearly got your children finished, and so well finished? Or are you one of these mothers who wants to keep her brood with her? I think it will be lovely when mine go out into the world."

And then they went to Africa.

Pauline had first written of the African trip in the spring of 1933, when Ernie and Bumby were in Havana. Pauline had returned with Patrick and Gregory to Key West. "Ernest is going to Africa some time this year," she wrote, "but so far the date isn't known, some time in the fall, I think." First, in the summer, they were going to Spain.

Pauline mentioned "Leicester's triumph." She had read a magazine story of Les's that Mother had sent and was sending it on to Ernie. Wasn't Mother a "diversified mother," said Pauline, "in the sense of diversified farmer (expression, a bit vague, but trust you to get my meaning)."

She also asked for a letter from me: "We haven't had much news from Sunny these days. Too bad, as she is a noble letter writer."

The next letter came from Tanganyika.

They had been on safari, and she wrote about it, but first she asked about Mother. They had heard of Mother's "double misfortune, breaking a leg and pneumonia." They were concerned. Pauline felt that Mother had been "awfully brave to write us those fine letters." She also thanked Marcelline for keeping them advised.

Ernie, she said, had heard from Leicester. His letter had been "full of fine hopes and enthusiasms . . . it is evidently a very exciting thing to be a young man going out into the world."

But their world was exciting then, too. Pauline found the African life "enchanting." The people were attractive and the country beautiful. "We have been out on Safari a month," she wrote, "and Ernest and I both got beautiful lions." Ernie had also gotten buffalo, leopard, buck, and a variety of birds. But then he had come down with dysentery and they had had to return to "civilization" until he was completely cured. They were planning to leave that day, said Pauline, for "another three weeks." Though the dysentery had "thinned him considerably," Ernie was well again and "the outdoor life had made him hard as nails."

36
Correspondents

All through the 1930s, as Ernie's fame spread throughout the world, my brother and I wrote each other regularly. Periodically, I would write him about the way things were going at home, and just as regularly he'd respond with advice and news from his area.

Ernie regarded me as his ambassador in the family court. Even earlier, he'd usually written me when he had special news. I had been the first one he wrote about his plan to marry Pauline, and had asked me then that I keep the secret until he wished to tell it. Because I always stuck up for him amid family criticism, my loyalty was unquestioned. I will always be proud of that.

On October 6, 1931, he wrote some pointed advice in answer to a letter from me telling him that out of a clear sky, Mother had requested that I contribute a third of my income earned as a doctor's assistant. She appreciated what I did around the house—shopping for groceries, keeping the car running, and being available for her many errands and appointments—but she wanted more cash.

Soon after Dad died in 1928, Ernest and Pauline had established a trust fund for Mother that would supposedly take care of her for the rest of her life. But the banking officials administering the trust had unfortunately, as I understood it, invested in the government bonds of some of the smaller European nations. In the stock market crash, these bonds had gone the way of many other securities. Mother was left with a good deal less income than she'd counted on.

Ernie pointed out that there was no similarity between my situation and that of other of my friends who might be living at home while working. Ours was a somewhat different fix because of Dad's bad luck. The way he saw it, I

Two photos of Ernest with trophies.

would be sensible to chip in what I could without it destroying my sense of making something for myself and having certain pleasures and the things I needed. It was my habit to save for trips, thinking this a way to contribute to my education.

Ernie gave me the details of the creation of a trust fund. Should Mother ever die—and he hoped she wouldn't ever—he was providing a sum for me that would be more than I would probably save in the next ten years if I were to bank regularly what I was contributing to the family. Ernie told me not to say anything about this. He asked me to save whenever I had the chance, because in his judgment I would eventually need savings, but also to put in what I could toward the family support for the time being. This would definitely help relieve the situation.

Ernie wrote gloomily about the way he had been going with his own profits. Confiding in me, he said that the last year, he had paid out more than 88 percent of what he had made, and that the dramatized version of *A Farewell to Arms* had not been much of a financial success. The film rights, however, ought to bring in a really substantial sum when all the details had been worked out.

A photo Ernie sent us. On the back he wrote: "My big lion (2nd). Broke his neck with a 220 gun, 30-06 at 40 yards. 1 shot."– Jan. 1934.

A later letter announced that he was having nothing at all to do with the moving picture. No doubt, he said, they'll have Catherine give birth to the American flag and rename the movie *The Star Spangled Banner.*

In a letter written from Key West just before Christmas in 1934, Ernie enclosed Christmas gift checks for each member of the family, for me to distribute. He also enclosed a letter to Mother for me to read and give to her. And he asked me to write him again, using Pauline's Piggott, Arkansas, address, as he had asked a great many questions.

In particular, Ernie wanted to know what news the family had had from our kid brother, Leicester, who had gone cruising down the Cuban coast in an eighteen-foot sailboat he had built with a friend. Les had adventures of his own that year, on far less money than a year of college would have cost.

Ernest wanted to know what had happened to "the Baron." He said that he and Pauline had had Les around Key West for something over three months that summer, and that Les had grown steadily more human. Now, Ernie explained, he had a soft spot in his heart for "the Baron," had really gotten fond of him, finally. However, he still wished the Baron would learn to wash.

Ernie called Les "the Baron" after somebody once asked him what his brother did, and Ernie—stopping the questioner in his tracks—replied that he thought everybody knew that "my brother's a baron." Now everybody around there believed Les was one.

Ernest was also curious for news of Carol. He commented on what I had reported in a recent letter about Carol and her husband, Jack, homesteading some land in central Florida. He was glad to hear Jack was back on the "papaya farm," and did I know, he asked, what papaya meant in Spanish. In Cuba, they call it fruta bomba, he said. He thought it tough on old Beefish and not necessarily nicer just because she liked it. As for him, he said, it wasn't any skin off his papaya, and a good many nights he had stayed awake right through not worrying about it.

I have lived to have a fine regard for Carol's husband, but Ernie never gave him a chance; they were very different people. As I think back, I don't believe any man would have seemed good enough for our darling little sister Carol. She was such a favorite.

Then Ernie did a parody on Cole Porter's "You're the Top"— though he said it was a swell record anyway. That is the one Cole Porter sings himself, with "Thank You So Much Mrs. Lounsburough Whitney" on the other side. Ernie told me to get the record, or he'd have to send it to me.

He said in his letter that the present yuletide spirit, the old golden Yuletide, was softening him up to plant a chaste kiss on my wrinkled forehead, and a swift kick to my rear; I was the greatest harpist since the Coolidge era.

He closed with the greatest of Christmas cheer to everybody, saying that someday when he was dead, he would answer all my fine letters—that because I wrote a damn good letter, it made him more ashamed of being such a lousy correspondent. Even so, he sent much love.

He signed himself as my "ancient Bro. Ernie."

All of Ernie's letters were a treat. He never worried about spelling or punctuation, because as he said, "You can always hire someone to do that."

37
"Mother Gracie"

Mother had insisted on maintaining her independence as long as she was able to do so. She would consent to "visit" her children, but preferred to think she could live in her own home, with or without domestic help, until her death.

She had always wanted to handle her own affairs, and on January 1, 1931, had written me her "will," prefacing it with a short note that it was to be used "only in case of [her] death" and returned to her when she asked for it. She stated:

> I hereby give to my daughter Madelaine all of my personal property in the house at 600 N. Kenilworth Ave. for her to divide among the 6 children or dispose of as she sees fit.

This was replaced, as many wills followed.

I had married Kenneth Mainland and had a son, Ernest Hemingway Mainland. When my husband and Young Ernie and I moved to Memphis, we looked forward to Mother's visits in the winter. She would only spare us a couple of weeks when she was well, as she had art pupils, lecturing engagements in many cities, and a constant round of social activities.

Wherever Mother went, she was treated royally. She treasured the newspaper clippings of her "triumphs"—as she referred to them. She was egotistical about her abilities, and rightly so. In interviews with the press, Mother spoke lovingly and proudly of her son Ernest, though she had been disappointed in his subject matter in the early years. But Mother did not rely for interest on being Ernest Hemingway's mother, and any reporter could find that out quickly. She also spoke proudly of the talents of her other five children. Newspaper articles brought out how interesting Mother was in her own right.

She was a delight and an inspiration to all who were privileged to know her. She "mothered" significant numbers of people, and many who admired her called her "Mother Hemingway."

In later years, after an unfortunate accident at an Oak Park hospital, in which—on the day before she would have been released— she sustained a cruel blow on the back of her head when an attendant mishandled her wheelchair, Mother's memory was greatly impaired. Mother Gracie was never the same.

On her last visit to us in Memphis in 1951, she seemed not to know who I was. I thought possibly she was playing a game with me, and so consulted our family doctor.

Dr. Clarke asked her who I was: "Mrs. Hemingway, you know who this lady is, don't you?"

Mother answered promptly, in her most gracious way: "Of course, Doctor, indeed I do."

I said to Dr. Clarke, "Ask her who I am."

He did so, and she answered, "She's a lovely lady who is taking care of me."

"But, Mrs. Hemingway," said the doctor, "this is your daughter Madelaine, you call 'Sunny,' isn't she?"

"Well, Doctor," my mother said, "I just don't get that."

It was heartbreaking. From that time on I knew she was in the senile dementia sickness we dreaded. She would hide from me like a child, and it was impossible to keep day help, or later nurses around the clock, to watch her.

One night, when Mother was especially restless, I called Dr. Clarke to our home. Our minister had called earlier and had been unable to soothe her troubled nerves. When Dr. Clarke came in the evening, I asked Mother to play the piano for him. She was in her nightgown, but she willingly sat at the piano.

Evidently her subconscious mind took over, as she was able to play, with great gusto, parts of several classical numbers. She modulated beautifully into many harmonious gems from her own compositions, long unplayed.

Dr. Clarke said that if he had not heard it himself, he never would have believed it possible for one in her demented state to perform so beautifully. Kenneth and I were so proud of her ability.

This therapy worked wonders for her for the time being, and she went peacefully to bed and rested well the rest of the night, while we made arrangements for her hospitalization.

Ernest kept in touch with me by letter all along, and appreciated the care I was able to give Mother. He wrote how much he appreciated my loving care of her, as he was unable even to attempt it.

When Mother's care had seemed too much to bear, I'd written brother Ernest in Havana, among others, asking that if he was "holding anything against her," to please forgive her so she might die in peace. I believe that when people are held on earth in sickness or mental torment for long periods, after having led useful, productive lives, someone, somewhere, holds harsh animosity toward them. These souls could be released through forgiveness. Prolonging the life of one who is through living only punishes the innocent who have the care and burden of him.

I have shared my belief with many friends since, and the response has been remarkably prompt. Surely to forgive, and to be forgiven, is a safe experiment.

Not long after Ernest received that letter in Havana, Mother Gracie died in her sleep in a hospital.

38
Havana, 1948

Back in 1948, when my son, Ernie Mainland, was ten years old, he and I had flown to Havana from our home in Memphis for a planned four-day visit with Ernest and his fourth wife, Mary.

We'd been in regular touch over the years. Often Ernie corresponded by cable, especially on important occasions. When my son had been born, Ernie cabled his congratulations to my husband Kenny and me, and to his godson. He would be writing, he said, and sending combination presents for our wedding, birthday, Christmas, and Fourth of July. He also immediately cabled me once in 1946 when he heard I was ill, saying he was sorry and that I should get well soon.

I looked forward to this trip—and it was a joyous time for us all. After being met at the airport by Ernie's chauffeur and ushered through customs with dispatch, we were driven out to the Finca in San Francisco de Paula. The big gate that held the sign saying, "No Admittance, no matter who you are," was swung open for our car to enter the lovely grounds of the Hemingway home.

Such natural beauty all around! A gorgeous specimen of an orchid, growing majestically on a tree near the front entrance, caught my eye immediately.

In the intervening years, Ernie and Pauline had been divorced and he'd married and then been divorced from Martha Gellhorn. His new wife, Mary, greeted us warmly, and I was handed a tumbler of what seemed to me straight gin. Brother Ernest, she said, was down at the swimming pool.

Young Ernie ran down to find him.

It was a happy greeting for all of us. For much too long my son had heard about his famous uncle, but he did not really know him.

We were shown our room in the guest cottage, and a maid was assigned to unpack for me. I spoke no Spanish and she no English. Her unpacking seemed very unnecessary to me, considering my sparse belongings, but I got nowhere trying to insist I could manage very well by myself.

Later in the afternoon, champagne was served to us and to two guests who had the privilege of dropping in. One guest was a famous jai alai player, greatly admired, I gathered.

At dinner, traditionally served at a late hour for us, wine was served at each place. I asked Ernest, "What about the boy drinking wine?"

"Wine's fine for him," Ernie said. "But don't give him hard liquor until he's thirteen."

We all laughed heartily.

At that time, they had a Chinese cook and Ernest ate his meal with chopsticks.

Young Ernie called him "Uncle Ernie." Ernest called the boy "Little Uncle Ernie." That title stuck in letters for many years.

Before the meal was finished that evening, I had to be excused to take the

boy to bed. He was dozing off periodically, though trying to enjoy his meal and the wine.

Both Young Ernie and I were fascinated with the household of cats. The bedroom between the living room and the veranda was the cat room. A couple of single beds and cushions were strewn about, as well as eating and drinking dishes to accommodate the scores of cats that kept accumulating. The room had a door that would swing in and out so the cats could come and go at their pleasure, day or night. Cases of salmon were fed to them.

The cats seemed to own the house, and we marveled at the patience everyone had with them. It was not at all unusual, time and again, to have to scatter cats from the breakfast table. The family dogs seemed much better behaved.

Ernest in Havana with sons Patrick and Gregory (by Pauline Pfeiffer) and John Hadley.

Two photos of Ernest Miller Hemingway with nephew Ernest Hemingway Mainland– "Uncle Ernie" and "Little Uncle Ernie," 1948.

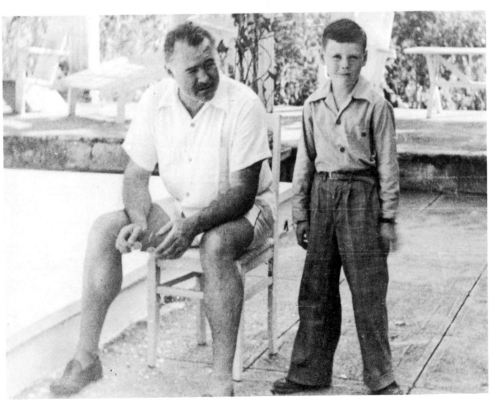

The day after we arrived, a trip was planned on Ernest's boat, the *Pilar*. It was a windy day, but the chance to go on the water might not come again, so we set out for the cove where the *Pilar* was moored.

After a drink at the nearby bar, we headed off on the rough sea. I could hear Uncle Ernie and Little Uncle Ernie having fun up top, but I couldn't see them from the lower deck, where I was "confined." (The Cuban maid, evidently misunderstanding something I had said when she was unpacking for me, had taken my only spare underpants. With the captain and Mary's lady guest below, I wasn't about to climb that ladder in the wind in a skirt!)

When lunchtime came, we put into a calm bay, and while the captain prepared a delicious dove pie and salad, we all passed the wineskin. Mary's friend and I were instructed in the knack of playing a fine stream of the wine, under slight pressure, to the back of the tongue, swallowing periodically. I hoped not to make a mess of myself publicly. But Ernest glowed with pride and said I was a true Hemingway when it came to swigging wine.

The day we went down to the town part of Havana, Ernest pointed out the interesting spots and bought me a big alligator handbag as a parting gift.

It had been a memorable visit.

Christmas card sent from Havana by Ernest and Mary.

39
Plane Crash

One Sunday morning in Petoskey, news came of Ernest's airplane crash in Africa. He was reported killed. I got the news from a gas station employee.

My dear friend, Elizabeth Harris Aerne, who lived in Oak Park, was contacted by Fannie Butcher of the *Chicago Tribune* for help in locating any members of the Hemingway family. Betty told her that Ernest's favorite sister, Sunny, lived in Petoskey, Michigan, and gave her my married name. Soon afterward newspapers from four states were trying to find me for information and comment.

Young Ernie and I were living in a rented apartment for our first winter as widow and son. Friends and neighbors came to call immediately. The minister came to comfort us. It was a gruesome and bewildering Sunday.

In one telephone interview, I said that I didn't believe Ernie was dead, that if anyone could get out of the crash, Ernie could. The *Chicago Tribune* promised to call me at any hour if they got further news. The next day—at 4:00 A.M.—they called to say Ernie was alive, though hurt. Young Ernie and I danced for joy.

My cable of congratulation to Ernest in Africa brought an appreciative cable in return.

40
Ernest John Miller

In 1956, after three and one-half years of being a widow with a young son, I found a fine man named Ernest John Miller. His wife had died a year after my husband, Kenneth Mainland. We met in a lawyer's office where I was working, and our friendship grew rapidly. We were married August 9 on the beach at Windemere.

Ernest Hemingway Mainland as a student in Phoenix, Arizona.

Sunny and Ernie Miller at Windemere.

Brother Ernie was relieved to know I had found a good man to take care of me and Young Ernie. He couldn't come to the wedding, so he paid for my sister Ursula to come to be my attendant. My son gave me away.

My brother Ernie and my husband Ernie never got to know each other. They would have been congenial as both were ardent sportsmen—tough, tender, and talented. Several times I tried to get them together with the excuse of delivering paintings that Ernie had designated me to choose for him at the time of Mother's funeral in River Forest, Illinois. But something always kept us apart.

Now, to distinguish between his own father and his stepfather, Young Ernie speaks of Kenneth as his Father and Ernie Miller as his Dad.

In 1969, Ernie Miller and I bought a home in Florida for the winter months. On February 5, 1972, he had a fatal coronary. I'm glad he lived to see Ernie Mainland marry and to enjoy being a grandfather. Judy Mainland bore a fine son named John Kenneth Mainland on September 1, 1969.

41
Ernest's Death

On July 2, 1961, the news of Ernest's death was verified by a telephone call from his friend Pappy Arnold in Ketchum, Idaho.

We had few of the intimate details that later came out, but my beloved brother Ernie was dead; that was definite and that's all that mattered to me. I was deeply shaken.

My son Ernie and I made immediate plans to get from Petoskey as far as Grand Rapids that day by car. Even after telephoning Les, Carol, and Marcelline, we were packed and out of the cottage on Walloon Lake before too many friends or any newspapers could get to us. We would fly the next day to Ketchum. Andy Kan arranged this.

My husband Ernie Miller took our dog Prince and fled to our Wolverine home. But once there he realized that our cottage would suddenly become irresistible to news people and curiosity seekers. That evening he made the thirty-mile trip back to Windemere to check windows, doors, and boats. Everything seemed in order, but when we returned after the funeral, my bedroom window was slightly open, and it was clear that the place had been investigated. When we returned, we were shown two very fine new pictures of the cottage that had been in the local paper, both lakeside and roadside views. I didn't dare report the theft of two first editions because I feared drawing further attention to the house.

For the funeral, my son Ernie and I met my sister Ursula at the Salt Lake City airport; she had come from Honolulu and was already being hounded by newsmen who had been notified of her flight plans.

To my son belongs the credit that we avoided the newsmen in the airport until our plane left for Ketchum. The ladies' room got pretty tiresome, but it was better than being photographed and questioned about a death of which we knew so little.

Bumby and others met us at the Ketchum area airport, and we drove to the house where Mary greeted Ura, Young Ernie, and me warmly. Morbidly, I looked around for signs of the tragedy that had happened the day before. Nothing! Not a sign of disorder, stain, or even a mar that I could see!

While Mary showed us through the house as though we were on a tour, I wondered if what we had been told could be true. We didn't dare ask any questions. Everything was in perfect order. We were invited to dinner and later loaned a car for the drive from the Christiana Motel where we were all staying.

Later we returned. We were served drinks, and while we talked, Ernie Mainland noticed someone outside the fence. It was a photographer, shooting through our window, evidently with a telescopic lens. Ernie drew the drapes and went out to have a word or two with the man.

Many phone calls came to the house while we were there. Piles of telegrams and rarer letters, arrived. I commented on a beautiful big flower arrangement in the living room, and Mary said it had come from Gary Cooper's widow, a dear friend. There seemed to be constant action, with decisions being made as to who should be met and who should be discouraged from coming to the funeral.

I was still in a state of shock so this part of our visit remains very vague. But I remember Mary talking spiritedly about funeral plans. Did Ursula and I think it enough to have a Catholic priest do a graveside service only, and so on? Of course, we agreed it was up to her to decide.

There was to be a delay of a day or two waiting for Ernest's son Patrick to arrive. Les and Gregory (Patrick's younger brother) had come together on the plane from Florida. Marce had come on her own. Carol had decided not to come, but to be with us in spirit and stay in the background, avoiding the publicity that was gathering momentum every minute.

I believed what I wanted to believe. I had to. I needed to comfort myself. Remembering that Ernie had been a sleepwalker in his youth, as I had been, it seemed possible that he had walked in his sleep . . . . I later saw how medication for my late husband's hypertension drastically altered his outlook and disposition. Had Ernie's medications influenced his actions? There were many possibilities. I had not seen him in a number of years. I did not know the state of his mind, the effect of all the accidents he'd had over the years.

It was painful how each person there was so emotionally controlled—

The Episcopal church in Ketchum where I read the burial service for Ernest before the graveside Catholic service that morning. I knelt in the fourth pew on the right.

outwardly. We seemed to be trying, always, not to let townspeople or sightseers know who we were when we went out of our rooms. But I am sure we fooled no one.

The holiday crowd continued its merriment, adding a slightly surrealistic touch to the sad days.

We drove around the area to see some of the sights, biding our time until we were told what to do and when to do it. Ernest's old friends in the town tried to entertain us, but we were numb. I had only an empty, floating feeling.

The morning of the funeral, I walked across the street from the motel to the small Episcopal church I had spotted. The building was empty. The light through the stained glass window behind the altar was beautiful. I hoped I could find some peace here. Some peace, at last.

I knelt down. I prayed. And I began to read, in breaking whispers, the entire burial service from the prayer book.

Before I got off my knees, I glanced down at the carpet. On the carpet was a perfect outline of Ernest's head, beard and all! It seemed as if his sad eyes were pleading.

I told myself, "Watch it, girl! Don't get carried away."

I told myself not to believe what I saw.

I looked again and the face was still there.

I went two pews forward, knelt there, and looked down at the carpet. There was nothing. Relieved, I went back to the pew where I had been before.

Ernest's face was still there: it was not a vague but a vivid outline.

Putting my finger to my lips, I planted a kiss of goodbye on his face—and as I did so, the apparition disappeared. The experience had been beautiful—powerful though frightening.

Very nearly in tears, I went back to the motel to tell Ura. She reluctantly went back to the church with me, walked to the same pew, and looked. We saw nothing.

I was afraid to tell anyone else about my experience for fear they would think I was cracking up. But I told my minister, Father Dudley Burr, when I returned to Petoskey. He was comforting and reassuring. He said such things certainly do happen. And my family doctor, my husband, and my son all understood—and comforted me.

The funeral was a nightmare! We had been issued handwritten "entrance permits" to the cemetery. Only an invited group was allowed inside the gates, but the television and radio men were within our hearing as we lined up at the grave.

"Entering now is his sister, Mrs. Ernest John Miller, with her son, Ernest Hemingway Mainland," I heard them announce.

The stage whispers continued and the summer heat bore down on us. One young acolyte assisting the priest fell to the ground in a dead faint during the short service.

We were not invited nor expected to sit in on the reading of the will. The many loyal, close friends of Ernest dispersed as quickly as possible. My son and I left still not knowing any details of Ernest's death. I still comforted myself, believing what I wanted to believe.

Ernest Hemingway's grave at Ketchum, Idaho. This photo was taken soon after the funeral—1961.

42
Memories

Since Ernest's death, a beautiful memorial to him has been placed in Sun Valley, Ketchum, Idaho, engineered by his widow Mary.

Here in Petoskey, at the Emmanuel Episcopal Church, I have donated in his memory a window depicting the Nativity.

In 1968, the Secretary of the Interior, Stuart Udall, designated our cottage "Windemere" a "National Historic Landmark." I accepted the bronze plaque with the understanding that it did not have to be displayed, and that this summer home would not be open to the public.

Many years ago our parents had the unique idea of planting and naming balsam trees on our property at Windemere for each child. The tallest was Marcelline, the next Ernest, and so on. These were planted in the area between the main house and the boathouse. Later Ursula's and then my trees joined the group, then Carol's and Les's trees. All but one of the trees are still there. They remind me of earlier days, of my sisters Ursula and Marcelline who have died, and of my brother Ernie.

The open field part of our yard, used at one time as a garden area, has since been planted with trees. One birch tree grew up as a volunteer from seed. This birch, which I protected from being plowed under during the gardening years, has since been dedicated to Brother Ernest, a self-made man. The two maples that I picked up along Indian Garden Road during road improvement time have been dedicated to Mother and Dad.

When the Kenilworth Avenue home was retenanted, the new people took off the music room entirely to eliminate a difficult heating problem. I visited it once later and was sickened to find cars parked in the yard, refrigerators in the halls, and every room used for roomers. It was worse than a gypsy camp!

Since that time, someone with taste has made it into a duplex, its respectability renewed and appreciated. Our Oak Park Avenue home, where four of the six children were born, is still kept up, and still has the dignity I think it deserves. Markers were placed on these two sites at the festivities for the seventy-fifth anniversary of Ernie's birth on July 21, 1974. I unveiled the birthplace marker and my son unveiled the marker at 600 North Kenilworth.

Ernest requested me early in his success as a writer not to send all my friends' and neighbors' copies of his books to him to autograph. The time involved in writing appropriate lines, and then all the addressing and having to see the books mailed off, was a chore he couldn't realize, he said. I respected

Memorial window for Ernest in Emmanuel Episcopal Church, Petoskey, Michigan.

his wish. Consequently, I have no autographed copies of his books, while absolute strangers—some of whom soft-soaped him into autographing many copies—boast a valuable collection.

Here at Walloon Lake our good friends try to preserve privacy for us. They do not tell visitors just where the Hemingway cottage is located. But many persevere and drop by. These admirers are professors of English, students, writers, would-be writers, newspapermen, and the like. Some say they just want to walk on the ground where Hemingway walked, and see what he saw from the shore.

The mantelpiece at Windemere with Mother's painting of Ernest.

Ernie playing "kick the can."

At times I have been kind, and talkative, to such interesting visitors. Sometimes I've even taken them to where the old Indian camp was located, though there's nothing of it to be seen now. But years later, an article would come out showing that those to whom I had been especially gracious had rewarded me with details of my own brand of lingo that could not have been repeated unless they had tape recorded my conversation secretly. Or worse, misquoted me! Less and less have I been able to trust visitors with the recollections they would love to hear.

Wherever else he went in the world—to Europe, Africa, Key West, Havana, Idaho—Ernie always remembered Walloon Lake and Windemere with affection. It was here he lived and gathered the material that would make his first stories, here that he vowed to be " 'fraid of nothing."

It was here, too, that I knew my brother best—in the long summers when we tramped the fields and enjoyed the lake together.

Those days were more than sixty years ago, but at times they are as bright and vivid to me as the foliage across the lake on a bright autumn day.

Left: Sunny at organ with Ernest Hemingway's picture above. Mother painted the picture from a photo. The sheet music of "Lovely Walloon" is by G.H.H. Hemingway. (Photo by Elizabeth Aerne.)

Below: Ernie Mainland unveiling the marker at 600 North Kenilworth Avenue, July 21, 1974.

Sunny holding commemorative plaque for Windemere.

Above, left: Photo of the Pilar *on Christmas card from Cuba. Ernest wrote, "Merry Christmas, Nunbones, to you and Ken and Uncle Ernie. Yr. Bro. Stein."*

Below: The Windemere shoreline.

Appendix-Library Lists

The library at Windemere included the following items:

Lulu's Library   Louisa May Alcott
The Reign of Law   James Lane Allen
Anthony Adverse   Hervey Allen
Mr. Munchausen   John Kendrick Bangs
John Fedder's Wife   Amelia E. Barr
The Old World in the New Century
      William E. Barton, D.D.
The Professor   Charlotte Bronte
Collected Poems of Rupert Brooke
Young Mrs. Jardine   Bullock
Mistress and Maid   Bullock
Byron's Complete Poetical Works
The Shadow of a Crime   Hall Caine
Pilgrims of the Plains   Kate A. Caplington
From Father to Son   Chellis
Sunny Ducrow   Henry St. John Cooper
Twelve volumes of James Fenimore Cooper
A Gentleman of Courage   James Oliver Curwood
Stories for Boys   Richard Harding Davis
The Flamingo Feather   Rene De Veaux
The Brothers Karamazov   Fyodor Dostoevsky
Magnificent Obsession   Lloyd C. Douglas
The Sign of the Four   Sir Arthur Conan Doyle
The Haunted Pajamas   Francis Perry Elliott
The Brewer's Family   Ellis
The Home Beyond, or Views of Heaven
      Samuel Fallows, D.D.
Beautiful Stories About Jesus   Canon Farrar, D.O.
The Meaning of Prayer   Henry Emerson Fosdick
Boy Life on the Prairie   Hamlin Garland
Cranford   Elizabeth Gaskell
Biography of a Prairie Girl   Eleanor Gates
Gray's Elegy   Thomas Gray
Rainbow Trail   Zane Gray
Our Country at War and Foreign Relations
      Murat Halstead
Alone   Harland
The Home of Shakespeare
      Watercolor sketches by Harlow, 1894

Wonder Book   Nathaniel Hawthorne
Sixes and Sevens   O. Henry
On a Slow Train Through Arkansas   T.W. Jackson
Three Men in a Boat   Jerome K. Jerome
The Idle Thoughts of an Idle Fellow
      Jerome K. Jerome
The Rubaiyat of Omar Khayyam
The Thread of Flame   Basil King
In the Eastern Seas   W.H. Kingston
Essays of Elia and Eliana   Charles Lamb
Lux Christi   Caroline Atwater Mason
Renascence   Edna St. Vincent Millay
Canoe Mates: Florida Reef and Everglades   Munroe
Daybreak in the Dark Continent   Wilson Naylor
Collected Poems 1897-1907   Henry Newbolt
Mr. Grex of Monte Carlo   E. Phillips Oppenheim
Ruth Erskin's Crosses   Pansy
Private Peat   Harold R. Peat
The Fourth Norwood   Robert E. Pinkerton
Book of Conundrums   Greta Robinson
Mornings in Florence   John Ruskin
Lady of the Lake   Sir Walter Scott
The Minister's Wooing   Harriet Beecher Stowe
Anna Karenina   Leo Tolstoy
Ten Volumes of *Stories by American Authors* 1896
Ten Volumes of *Stories by English Authors* 1896
Masterpieces of Adventure (4 vols.): Sea and Sky et al.
New Elementary Agriculture
Boy Scouts of America Handbook
Three Kingdoms: Handbook of Agassiy Association
Holy Bible (King James Version)
Days with the Great Composers
Christmas Carols
Young Folks Library of Choice Literature
The Victor Book of Operas
Seven volumes of old books from Dad's medical library
Grandfather Ernest Hall's Episcopal Prayer Book
Old copies of Oak Park, Illinois, Weekly *Oak Leaves*
Chatterbox (1884)

The library at the Oak Park Avenue house included the following items:

Winesburg, Ohio   Sherwood Anderson
Pride and Prejudice   Jane Austen
Droll Stories   Balzac
Looking Backward   Edward Bellamy
The Way of All Flesh   Samuel Butler
Tobacco Road   Erskine Caldwell
Alice in Wonderland   Lewis Carroll
Don Quixote   Cervantes
Plays   Anton Chekhov
Lord Jim   Joseph Conrad
Red Badge of Courage   Stephen Crane
Two Years Before the Mast   Richard Henry Dana
Robinson Crusoe   Daniel Defoe
Set of Charles Dickens:
      David Copperfield, Oliver Twist, et al.
Three Soldiers   John Dos Passos
An American Tragedy   Theodore Dreiser
Sister Carrie   Theodore Dreiser
The Three Musketeers   Alexander Dumas
The Sound and the Fury   William Faulkner
Madame Bovary   Gustave Flaubert
Tess of the D'Urbervilles   Thomas Hardy
The Scarlet Letter   Nathaniel Hawthorne
The Hunchback of Notre Dame   Victor Hugo
A Doll's House   Henrik Ibsen
Short Stories   Washington Irving
The Portrait of a Lady   Henry James
A Portrait of the Artist as a Young Man
      James Joyce
Kim   Rudyard Kipling
Dodsworth   Sinclair Lewis
Death in Venice   Thomas Mann
The Garden Party   Katherine Mansfield
Moby Dick   Herman Melville
The Past Recaptured   Marcel Proust
Tragedies and Comedies   William Shakespeare
The Grapes of Wrath   John Steinbeck
Tortilla Flat   John Steinbeck
The Red and the Black   Stendahl
Dracula   Bram Stoker
Uncle Tom's Cabin   Hariett Beecher Stowe
Vanity Fair   William Thackeray
Candide   Voltaire
Fortitude   Hugh Walpole
The Age of Innocence   Edith Wharton
Leaves of Grass   Walt Whitman
The Picture of Dorian Gray   Oscar Wilde
Nana   Emile Zola
Swiss Family Robinson   Johann Wyss

Sets of O. Henry
Sets of Shakespeare
Sets of Book of Knowledge
Sets of *Author's Digest*
Sets of bird books (leather bound)
Sets of Henry Wadsworth Longfellow's works
Bound volumes of *St. Nicholas* Magazine
      (given to sister Carol)
Encyclopedias
Set of Alexander Pope
      (over 200 years old, given to Ernest's son John)
Set of Edgar Allen Poe
Set of Hawthorne

Unspecified titles by:
   Robert Benchley
   John Donne
   Ford Madox Ford
   Richard Halliburton
   Ring Lardner
   Jack London
   Henry Wadsworth Longfellow
   Dorothy Parker
   Ezra Pound
   Robert W. Service
   Gertrude Stein
   Booth Tarkington
   Henry David Thoreau
   Mark Twain